THE VICTORIAN FRAME OF MIND

Walter E. Houghton

"The most thorough and comprehensive study of its subject that has yet been written. . . . Here is a full and intelligent analysis of the different facets of that many-sided thing, the Victorian mind and soul. An important part ⟨of th⟩is analysis is the relating of one attitude ⟨or⟩ tendency to another, so that, although ⟨they⟩ are contradictory, the agreements and ⟨d⟩iscords and their causes are made intelli-⟨gible⟩. The analysis is supported everywhere ⟨by r⟩ich and often fresh documentation. Mr. Houghton writes with vigor and clarity. The book seems to me a large and solid contribution to the understanding of Victorian civilization and Victorian literature." — Douglas Bush

"In his preliminary notes, Mr. Houghton intimates that he has been at work on this book for some twenty-five or more years. The result is undoubtedly one of those rare and beautiful distillations of a long period of scholarship, of a saturation in the material, until the fortunate reader knows in every sentence that he is receiving the benefit of thousands and thousands of unquoted pages. I feel that this book is an essential work for every student of nineteenth-century New England and America; but more than this, I am persuaded that here is a study of immense significance in terms of method." — Perry Miller, *The New England Quarterly*

"Will undoubtedly become a standard for students of the Victorian Period." — *Books Abroad*

Printed in the U.S.A.

Into the Demon Universe

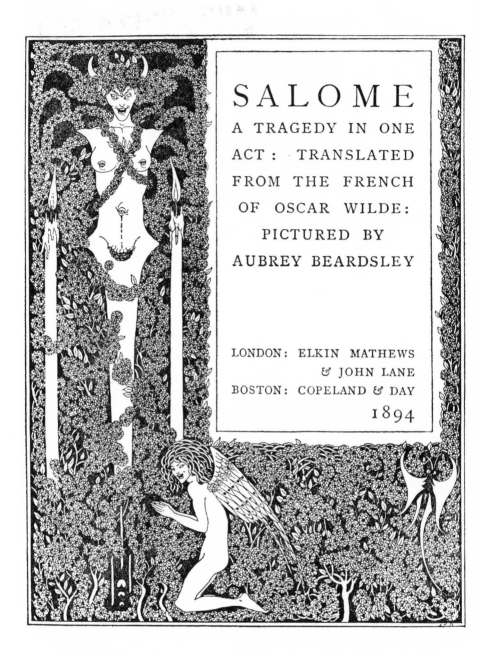

SALOME

A TRAGEDY IN ONE
ACT : TRANSLATED
FROM THE FRENCH
OF OSCAR WILDE:
PICTURED BY
AUBREY BEARDSLEY

LONDON: ELKIN MATHEWS
& JOHN LANE
BOSTON: COPELAND & DAY
1894

Title page for the original 1894 edition of *Salome*, designed by Aubrey Beardsley.

INTO THE DEMON UNIVERSE

A Literary Exploration of Oscar Wilde

Christopher S. Nassaar

New Haven and London, Yale University Press
1974

Library of Congress catalog card number: 73-86910
International standard book number: 0-300-01684-0

Designed by John O. C. McCrillis
and set in Baskerville type.
Printed in the United States of America by
The Vail-Ballou Press, Inc., Binghamton, N.Y.

Published in Great Britain, Europe, and Africa by
Yale University Press, Ltd., London.
Distributed in Latin America by Kaiman & Polon,
Inc., New York City; in Australasia and Southeast
Asia by John Wiley & Sons Australasia Pty. Ltd.,
Sydney; in India by UBS Publishers' Distributors Pvt.,
Ltd., Delhi; in Japan by John Weatherhill, Inc., Tokyo.

To the Memory of my Grandfather
Ferid Alexander Atiyeh, M.B.E.

All art is at once surface and symbol.

OSCAR WILDE, preface to
The Picture of Dorian Gray

Contents

Acknowledgments

I wish to thank greatly James G. Nelson of the University of Wisconsin. His insights into the 1890s were both a help and an inspiration to me while I was preparing the doctoral dissertation out of which this book grew. He also aided me immensely with his collection of rare nineties material, at a time when I was in Lebanon and isolated from a research library. My thanks go, too, to Alvin Whitley of the University of Wisconsin, for kindly offering valuable comments on how I might improve the original manuscript for publication. To Ian Fletcher of the University of Reading I owe a deep and special debt, for he generously guided me through the final revisions of the manuscript and saved me from committing several rash errors.

I would also like to express my deep gratitude to Jennifer Alkire of the Yale University Press. I shall always remember her encouragement and her warm enthusiasm for my manuscript. I am also very grateful to Merle Spiegel, who carried on where Mrs. Alkire left off, and to Barbara Folsom, who gave excellent editorial guidance. To all, I offer my thanks and best wishes.

C. S. N.

May 1973

Introduction

My purpose in writing this book on Oscar Wilde is twofold. The first aim is to provide an adequate analysis of Wilde's major works and thereby lay to rest the idea that he was a literary failure—or the more prevalent one that he is saved only by his wit. Wilde was the last of the great Victorians, and he deserves a place in literature like those accorded to Tennyson, Arnold, Dickens, Pater, George Eliot, and others. Hopefully, my book will reveal Wilde's true caliber and will stimulate further analysis of his works. Much remains to be done, and perhaps other approaches than mine will prove more rewarding. What makes this book necessary is the almost total absence of intelligent criticism on Wilde, a major literary figure. Apart from Richard Ellmann's essays, the available criticism on Wilde is neither perceptive nor engaging. With very few exceptions, moreover—San Juan's *The Art of Oscar Wilde* is the only notable one—all published full-length studies of Wilde to date are biographies. The importance and originality of the literature he produced has not yet been recognized.

My second aim in writing this book is to provide a key by which the decadent movement may be understood. The English literary decadence was the major artistic movement of the 1890s and Wilde was the dominant figure of this movement. In two of his works—*The Picture of Dorian Gray* and *Salome*—he offered an interpretation of decadence. The flow of his works as a whole, moreover, fits this interpretation extremely well—frighteningly well, in fact. Now that the decadent poets have begun to arouse genuine critical interest, my analysis of Wilde may perhaps prove valuable as a guide through the dark and fascinating maze of the 1890s. Karl Beckson has rightly noted, in the introduction to his anthol-

ogy, *Aesthetes and Decadents,* that "Wilde impresses us not
only as a symbol but a cipher by which the Nineties may be
read." [1]

Recently, the idea of the nineties as a close-ended phase has
been rejected and the emphasis has been on the connections
between the 1890s and the so-called modern period. Without
denying that such connections exist, I would like to shift the
emphasis back to the nineteenth-century aspects of the decadence and suggest that the movement's "modernity" is mar-
ginal. There is a line in Victorian literature whose chief figures are Rossetti, Pater, and Wilde. This line is deeply rooted
in the Romantic period, especially in the poetry of John Keats,
the most aesthetic of the Romantic poets. Demonism, moreover, is implicit, and often explicit, in Romanticism. The demonic world also surfaces at times in Rossetti—for instance,
in his painting of Jane Morris as Proserpina in the 1870s, in
his interest in Lilith, and in his poem, "The Orchard Pit."
Demonism is also very apparent in Pater, who found a strange
beauty in it.

Wilde continued and developed the Keats-Rossetti-Pater
tradition in nineteenth-century literature. Conscious of his
place at the end of a century, he elevated the demonic to the
status of a religion and tried to terminate the nineteenth century with a religion of evil, an unholy worship of evil beauty.
Instead of the goddess of *Endymion* or Rossetti's blessed
damozels, Wilde offered the Victorians the chillingly evil Salome as an erotic-divine object of worship. In his paintings
and literature, Rossetti had explored his own soul and found
it largely pure, though stained with evil. Pater, in *The Renaissance,* had regarded modern human nature as mostly evil and
had been fascinated by both the pure and evil strains reflected
in the portrait of the Mona Lisa. In *Salome,* Wilde went beyond Pater, presenting human nature—modern and ancient—
as entirely evil, and built a Satanic religion around the figure
of Salome—a religion devoted to the worship of evil beauty.
And he was ultimately destroyed by his religion.

1. Karl Beckson, introduction to *Aesthetes and Decadents,* ed. Karl
Beckson (New York: Vintage, 1966), p. xxxix.

I have not, in this book, attempted an exhaustive analysis of Wilde but have concentrated on his major works, studying the development of Oscar Wilde the decadent, who began by writing fairy tales and ended by declaring himself damned. Wilde seems to have undergone a basic change, both psychologically and as an artist, after his first homosexual experience in 1886, and his best work really dates from then. His literary productions in 1886 and after, moreover, constitute a new beginning, for he definitely regarded homosexual contact as evil and now wrote in full awareness of a demonic impulse within himself.

Wilde's early poems, published in volume form in 1881, are clearly second-rate and I have not offered an analysis of them. They are really exercises in imitation, showing how widely read their author is and revealing a chameleon-like quality in him, but no more. Nor can these early poems be regarded as the initial phase of Wilde's career. They are an inseparable part of the old Wilde—the boyish, carefree plagiarizer who suddenly disappeared from the scene late in 1886, yielding to the sin-conscious homosexual.

Wilde also wrote two plays during this early period. These are *The Duchess of Padua* and *Vera*. *The Duchess of Padua*, like the early poems, is an exercise in imitation, the work imitated being Shelley's *The Cenci*, which Wilde considered at the time to be the best play the nineteenth century had produced. Wilde in no way attempts to go beyond *The Cenci* in *The Duchess of Padua*, however, nor does he provide us with an entirely successful imitation. Practically all that can be said for *The Duchess of Padua* is that it is second-rate Shelley. *Vera*, a story about Russian nihilists, is perhaps relatively good melodrama, but it is no more than that. In a word, the basic fault of *Vera* is that it has no intellectual content. Had Wilde stopped writing before 1886, his work would have had no literary value to speak of.

1 The Fairy Tales

"Piper, sit thee down and write
In a book, that all may read."
So he vanish'd from my sight,
And I pluck'd a hollow reed,

And I made a rural pen,
And I stain'd the water clear,
And I wrote my happy songs
Every child may joy to hear.

BLAKE, introduction to
Songs of Innocence

1886—in that year Oscar Wilde died and was born anew. Shelley, in *Adonais,* speaks of "the contagion of the world's slow stain" (l. 356), and for Wilde this contagion began at the age of thirty-two, when he was seduced into homosexual practices by Robert Ross. Richard Ellmann rightly treats this event as pivotal both for Wilde the man and Wilde the artist. Suddenly, and at a remarkably late age, Oscar Wilde became seriously aware of the dark side of life, and suddenly the second-rate, highly imitative writer disappeared and Wilde began to produce original literature with a claim to immortality. To read his works chronologically is to discover that Wilde's vision darkened almost without interruption until it ended in despair.

We poets in our youth begin in gladness;
But thereof come in the end despondency and madness,
[ll. 48–49]

wrote Wordsworth in "Resolution and Independence," thereby summarizing in two lines a central problem in Romantic experience.

1

Wilde, the last of the nineteenth-century Romantics, faced this problem in his own way, and failed entirely to solve it. The process of age, of growing up, is one that opens the Romantic to the world's slow stain and immerses him in a black and soul-destroying universe. Wilde's literary productions during and after 1886 evince a deepening if jagged exploration of the demonic and a final shocked cry of despair. The life and the works reflect each other, but it is my purpose in this study to focus on Wilde's works and to keep his life in the background, insofar as this is possible. There are many biographies of Wilde. What is needed is an adequate study of the literature he produced.

"Lord Arthur Savile's Crime" is the first work to emerge out of what Richard Ellmann calls "the new Wilde" [1]—the Wilde who had succumbed to the homosexual impulse and had become interested in sin and crime. It is also Wilde's first important literary production and one of the most delightfully hilarious things he ever wrote. Much of the story's charm, however, lies in its rich, cleverly camouflaged intellectual content. The theme of the tale is foreshadowed in the very first paragraph:

> It was Lady Windermere's last reception before Easter, and Bentinck House was even more crowded than usual. Six Cabinet Ministers had come on from the Speaker's Levée in their stars and ribands, all the pretty women wore their smartest dresses, and at the end of the picture-gallery stood the Princess Sophia of Carlsrühe, a heavy Tartar-looking lady, with tiny black eyes and wonderful emeralds, talking bad French at the very top of her voice, and laughing immoderately at everything that was said to her. It was certainly a wonderful medley of people. Gorgeous peeresses chatted affably to violent Radicals, popular preachers brushed coat-tails with eminent sceptics, a

1. Richard Ellmann, "Introduction: The Artist as Critic as Wilde" in *The Artist as Critic: Critical Writings of Oscar Wilde,* ed. Richard Ellmann, p. xviii.

perfect bevy of bishops kept following a stout prima-
donna from room to room, on the staircase stood several
Royal Academicians, disguised as artists, and it was said
that at one time the supper-room was absolutely crammed
with geniuses. In fact, it was one of Lady Windermere's
best nights, and the Princess stayed till nearly half-past
eleven.[2]

The paragraph is a collection of opposites, wonderfully held
in balance, but unnaturally so. Lady Windermere's reception
cannot last forever, and with its end the delicate balance of
opposites will collapse and hostilities will resume between the
gorgeous peeresses and the violent radicals, the geniuses and
the demands of the stomach. The Princess Sophia is particularly worthy of notice. As a princess from a foreign land, wearing wonderful emeralds at a charming reception, she suggests
the beautiful, pure, and angelic. However, there is clearly
something savage and demonic about her. She looks like a
Tartar, has tiny black eyes, and behaves in an uncivilized manner, talking bad French and laughing immoderately. The
Princess Sophia is particularly important because she combines within herself two opposing strains, one pure and the
other demonic. In a possible allusion to Cinderella, Wilde has
her leave the reception shortly before midnight. Subtly and
unobtrusively, Wilde has suggested the main theme of his
story in the first paragraph.

We never learn what happens to Princess Sophia, but Lord
Arthur Savile also possesses two opposing strains in his character. The pure strain is reflected in his name. In the last
decades of the nineteenth century, *The Idylls of the King* was
an extremely well-known and very popular work, and the
name Arthur in a literary work tended to associate its possessor
with Tennyson's noble and totally pure King Arthur. Wilde

2. Oscar Wilde, *Lord Arthur Savile's Crime and Other Tales,* ed. Robert
Ross (London: Methuen, 1908), pp. 3–4. All future references to "Lord
Arthur Savile's Crime" are to this edition and are cited in parentheses in
the text. The story will be designated as "Crime."

makes this association more explicit by elevating his Arthur
to the rank of lord. Lord Arthur's high-sounding surname,
moreover, connects him with the earls of Savile and also suggests George Savile, who succeeded his father, Sir William, as
fourth baronet in 1644. A famous English politician, George
Savile was elevated to the peerage in 1668 as Baron Savile of
Eland and Viscount Halifax. In 1679, he was created earl of
Halifax and finally, in 1682, he became the first marquess of
Halifax. He died in 1695 and was succeeded by his son, with
whose death the peerage became extinct. Savile also suggests
Savile Row, an extremely fashionable London street known
for its tailor shops frequented by the aristocracy. Lord Arthur
Savile's impressive name, then, connects its tall, handsome
possessor with a realm that is pure, elevated, and exclusive.
Apparently, he is destined to exist in a world above and
separate from the ugly, evil things in life.

There is latent in Arthur, however, a strain that is quite
base. "Lord Arthur Savile's Crime" is about the coming-of-age
of Arthur. "I am not a child," he insists, and indeed he is engaged to be married. Marriage is a symbol of the transition
from boyhood to manhood, but this transition involves for
him the destruction of boyish innocence and the consequent
unpleasant confrontation with evil. In an amused, ironic tone,
Wilde reports Arthur's reaction as he first confronts the palm-
reader Podgers:

> He had lived the delicate and luxurious life of a young
> man of birth and fortune, a life exquisite in its freedom
> from sordid care, its beautiful boyish insouciance; and
> now for the first time he had become conscious of the ter-
> rible mystery of Destiny, of the awful meaning of Doom.
> ["Crime," p. 16]

Sybil, Arthur's beautiful fiancée, is a symbol incarnate of all
that is pure within Arthur, and his devotion to her is a symbolic devotion to an ideal of purity within himself. "Sybil was
to him a symbol of all that is good and noble" ("Crime,"
p. 28), Wilde informs us, and later on we are told that Arthur

"stopped at a florist's, and sent Sybil a beautiful basket of narcissus" ("Crime," p. 30). The fat and coarse Podgers, on the other hand—a groveler at the feet of the aristocracy [3]—is a symbol of all that is base and corrupt within Arthur. The evidence for this statement is, I feel, strong. When Podgers reads Lord Arthur's palm, he finds there not only Lord Arthur's future but his own as well. The streak of blood he finds embedded in Arthur's palm is Podgers's own blood. The only conceivable reason, moreover, why Lord Arthur cannot marry Sybil until he has murdered Podgers is because Podgers exists within Arthur and will destroy the marriage if it occurs: the principle of good cannot be totally possessed until the principle of evil is faced and destroyed within the self. The murder will be a form of self-purification for Arthur, and Podgers is well aware that he is to be the victim. Consider the following quotation:

> For a moment Lord Arthur had been tempted to play the coward's part, to write to Lady Clementina for the [poisoned] pill, and to let the marriage go on as if there was no such person as Mr. Podgers in the world. His better nature, however, soon asserted itself, and even when Sybil flung herself weeping into his arms, he did not falter. The beauty that stirred his senses had touched his conscience also. He felt that to wreck so fair a life for the sake of a few months' pleasure would be a wrong thing to do. ["Crime," p. 36]

Lord Arthur's baser nature tempts him cowardly to destroy Sybil "for the sake of a few months' pleasure," but "his better nature" soon asserts itself and he decides not to. As long as there is such a person as Mr. Podgers in the world, Arthur cannot marry Sybil without destroying her. The reason is that Podgers is an embodiment of Arthur's baser nature, existing

3. The duchess of Paisley reflects to herself that Podgers is a "cheiropodist"—a foot-reader. Before being introduced to him, she hopes that he is a foreigner, because "it wouldn't be quite so bad then."

within as well as outside him, though Arthur, at this stage, is too thoroughly innocent to recognize the fact. As Wilde reminds us at one point, "He was still very young."

But Arthur will destroy Podgers, as Podgers realizes at once upon seeing Lord Arthur's palm:

> When Mr. Podgers saw Lord Arthur's hand he grew curiously pale, and said nothing. A shudder seemed to pass through him, and his great bushy eyebrows twitched convulsively, in an odd, irritating way they had when he was puzzled. Then some huge beads of perspiration broke out on his yellow forehead, like a poisonous dew, and his fat fingers grew cold and clammy. ["Crime," p. 13]

Podgers, cornered, reveals all to Lord Arthur except the fact that it is he Arthur is destined to murder. "It will take a little time" for Arthur to discover this, and Podgers, "playing nervously with a flash watch-chain" ("Crime," pp. 18–19), knows this and finally manages to smile at Arthur's impatience.

Podgers's revelation plunges Lord Arthur into a terrible world, black and hideous:

> The night was bitter cold, and the gas-lamps round the square flared and flickered in the keen wind; but his hands were hot with fever, and his forehead burned like fire. . . . A policeman looked curiously at him as he passed, and a beggar, who slouched from an archway to ask for alms, grew frightened, seeing misery greater than his own. . . .
>
> Then he wandered across Oxford street into narrow, shameful alleys. Two women with painted faces mocked at him as he went by. From a dark courtyard came a sound of oaths and blows, followed by shrill screams, and, huddled upon a damp door-step, he saw the crooked-backed forms of poverty and eld. ["Crime," pp. 20–21]

Arthur does not remain long in this demonic underworld, however. As the dawn breaks, he sees a group of rustics coming

into London, and "rude as they were, with their heavy, hob-
nailed shoes, and their awkward gait, they brought a little of
Arcady with them" ("Crime," p. 24). Lord Arthur then goes
home, sleeps, and wakes to a new world:

> Never had life seemed lovelier to him, never had the
> things of evil seemed more remote. Then his valet brought him a cup of chocolate on a
> tray. After he had drunk it, he drew aside a heavy *por-
> tière* of peach-coloured plush, and passed into the bath-
> room. The light stole softly from above, through thin
> slabs of transparent onyx, and the water in the marble
> tank glimmered like a moonstone. He plunged hastily in,
> till the cool ripples touched throat and hair, and then
> dipped his head right under, as though he would have
> wiped away the stain of some shameful memory. When he
> stepped out he felt almost at peace. The exquisite physi-
> cal conditions of the moment had dominated him, as in-
> deed often happens in the case of very finely-wrought
> natures, for the senses, like fire, can purify as well as de-
> stroy. ["Crime," pp. 25-26]

Lord Arthur's bath is a symbolic baptism, an entry into a
world of beauty and purity higher than the one from which
he had fallen—"Never had life seemed lovelier to him, never
had the things of evil seemed more remote." He emerges from
the bath purified and "almost at peace." He is not totally at
peace, however, because he has not yet attained the highest
state of purification, the state that will allow him to marry
Sybil. He has faced Podgers and escaped from his world, but
Podgers still lives.

The rest of the story is largely a satire on the Victorian
sense of duty—indeed the story is subtitled "A Study of Duty."
Since Podgers is able to predict the future—and there is no
question about that—the future is obviously predetermined
and nothing can be done to alter it. Arthur never once doubts
the truth of Podgers's prediction of murder. Lord Arthur's
chief fault, however, is his extreme impatience. "Be quick," he

twice orders Podgers, causing the doomed man to smile, and
after learning that he has successfully murdered Podgers, he
dashes at full speed to Sybil:

> "My dear Sybil," cried Lord Arthur, "let us be married
> tomorrow."
> "You foolish boy! Why, the cake is not even ordered!"
> said Sybil, laughing through her tears.

VI

> When the wedding took place, some three weeks later.
> . . . ["Crime," pp. 58–59]

One cannot rush Providence, but Lord Arthur solemnly decides it is his duty to Sybil to do precisely that and commit
murder as soon as possible. Carlyle, in *Sartor Resartus* and
The French Revolution, had stated that the Divine Will unfolds itself in time and that it is man's duty to assist it. Of all
the Victorians, it was Carlyle who spoke the loudest of man's
duty. It is quite possible, then, that Wilde had Carlyle specifically in mind when he wrote "Lord Arthur Savile's Crime,"
and this is supported by Jane Percy's letter in the story. She
is the dean of Chichester's daughter, and one sentence in her
letter reads as follows: "Papa says Liberty was invented at the
time of the French Revolution. How awful it seems!"
("Crime," p. 52). Is the reference to the revolution itself or to
Carlyle's *The French Revolution?*

At the risk of straining the reader's credence, I would like to
suggest that it is probably the latter. Indeed, much of the
letter—it appears to me—seems to be a series of suppressed
comic jabs at Carlyle. For instance: "Thank you so much for
the flannel for the Dorcas Society, and also for the gingham. I
quite agree with you that it is nonsense their wanting to wear
pretty things, but everybody is so Radical and irreligious nowadays, that it is difficult to make them see that they should not
try and dress like the upper classes. I am sure I don't know
what we are coming to" ("Crime," p. 51). And again: "How

true, dear aunt, your idea is, that in their rank of life they should wear what is unbecoming. I must say it is absurd, their anxiety about dress, when there are so many more important things in this world, and in the next. I am so glad your flowered poplin turned out so well, and that your lace was not torn" ("Crime," pp. 52–53). And Jane goes on to talk about frills and bows and satins, as Wilde playfully retailors *Sartor Resartus* along dandiacal lines.

Lord Arthur, in pursuing what he considers to be his duty, only succeeds in tempting Providence, for he does not realize it is Podgers he must murder. This is the result of his listening to a false prophet, and therefore receiving the truth incomplete. As Lady Windermere observes, however, "Surely Providence can resist temptation by this time" ("Crime," p. 6). Luckily for Arthur, it can, and Lady Clementina dies a natural death despite his efforts. Arthur then sends an explosive clock to the dean of Chichester, but it blows up harmlessly, only knocking over the carving of the goddess of liberty, causing it to fall flat on its face and break its nose. Finally, Arthur despairs of success and comes to thoroughly identify destiny with doom, as he has been doing more or less throughout the tale. "We live in an age of unbelief," preaches the dean of Chichester, and Arthur is indeed an excellent example of the age in this respect. At any rate, he decides on total passivity:

He had made up his mind not to try any more experiments. Then he wandered down to the Thames Embankment, and sat for hours by the river. The moon peered through a mane of tawny clouds, as if it were a lion's eye, and innumerable stars spangled the hollow purple dome. Now and then a barge swung out into the turbid stream, and floated away with the tide, and the railway signals changed from green to scarlet as the trains ran shrieking across the bridge. After some time, twelve o'clock boomed from the tall tower at Westminster, and at each stroke of the sonorous bell the night seemed to tremble. Then the

railway lights went out, one solitary lamp left gleaming
like a large ruby on a giant mast, and the roar of the city
became fainter.
   At two o'clock he got up, and strolled towards Black-
friars. How unreal everything looked! How like a strange
dream! The houses on the other side of the river seemed
built out of darkness. One would have said that silver and
shadow had fashioned the world anew. The huge dome of
St. Paul's loomed like a bubble through the dusky air.
["Crime," pp. 55–56]

The first point to note about this passage is the emphasis
on time. The story is shot through with references to time and
clocks and watches. Now we have Big Ben itself announcing
the end of a day and the beginning of a new one. Before 12:00
P.M., Arthur's world is a beautiful but tainted one. It is dominated by the moon and an exquisite, star-spangled "hollow
purple dome"; but it also contains such disturbingly unaes-
thetic elements as barges, a turbid stream, and shrieking
trains. After 12:00 P.M., this world begins to fade away—lights
go out, the roar of the city grows faint—and an entirely fabu-
lous dreamworld of silver and shadow emerges, wrapped in the
religious aura of the huge, lofty dome of St. Paul's. The time
for his salvation has come: Arthur accidentally stumbles across
Podgers, the only remaining blot on the scene, and quickly
flings him into the Thames. "At last he seemed to have realised the decree of destiny. He heaved a deep sigh of relief, and
Sybil's name came to his lips" ("Crime," pp. 56–57).
   Finally, "Lord Arthur Savile's Crime" is also about two
forms of art. Podgers is an artist-figure, and he practices the
art of reading palms. He is at Lady Windermere's to perform,
and she associates him with other artists. Lady Windermere
complains that Podgers does not look "a bit like a cheiroman-
tist," then adds, "All my pianists look exactly like poets; and
all my poets look exactly like pianists" ("Crime," p. 7). Podgers's "art" is called a science, however, and he pursues it with
great objectivity, to the point of using a small magnifying

glass to study Lord Arthur's palm. Podgers's art, furthermore, deals with the dark, fallen side of life, and he makes his living by revealing people's sins and vices. All this suggests the naturalist artist—Zola, perhaps, or George Moore, whose novel *A Mummer's Wife* (1885) was "the first completely Naturalistic novel in English." [4] Podgers is the type of the fallen artist who deals with the fallen world.

Sybil counterbalances Podgers; she represents a pure, beautiful art that stands in opposition to naturalistic art, and is utterly untainted by the fallen world. Lord Arthur's devotion to her as a symbol of the highest spiritual state suggests the aesthetic artist—Rossetti, Poe, and others. In the 1880s Oscar Wilde was a prominent aesthete, and his story is a celebration of aestheticism and aesthetic art. In Greek mythology Sybil is Apollo's handmaiden, and Apollo is mainly the god of prophecy and the patron god of art. Though Wilde's Sybil has no prophetic powers, she does suggest aesthetic art in this tale, and the mythic roots of her name reinforce her connection with art. That Wilde was fully aware of the connotations of

4. Enid Starkie, *From Gautier to Eliot* (London: Hutchinson, 1962), p. 74. Wilde, though, probably regarded the appearance of Moore's "completely Naturalistic novel," *A Mummer's Wife*, more as the culmination of a movement in nineteenth-century English literature than the beginning of a new one.

In *The Decay of Lying*, Vivian, the main speaker, observes at one point: "Believe me, my dear Cyril, modernity of form and modernity of subject-matter are entirely and absolutely wrong. We have mistaken the common livery of the age for the vesture of the Muses, and spend our days in the sordid streets and hideous suburbs of our vile cities when we should be out on the hillside with Apollo. Certainly we are a degraded race, and have sold our birthright for a mess of facts." At another point, he says: "Mr. Ruskin once described the characters in George Eliot's novels as being like the sweepings in a Pentonville omnibus," then adds that "M. Zola's characters are much worse." Vivian makes a plea to stop "our monstrous worship of facts" before beauty passes away from the land. Wilde seems to have regarded George Eliot's novels as having strong affinities with the naturalist school, and his unsympathetic presentation of the Jewish theater-owner in *The Picture of Dorian Gray*—he is part of the hideous world of the naturalists—is possibly a jab at *Daniel Deronda*.

the name becomes clear when we read what he wrote about Elizabeth Barrett Browning in "English Poetesses," an article published in 1888: "She was a Sybil delivering a message to the world, sometimes through stammering lips, and once at least with blinded eyes, yet always with the true fire and fervour of a lofty and unshaken faith, always with the great raptures of a spiritual nature, the high ardours of an impassioned soul. As we read her best poems we feel that, though Apollo's shrine be empty and the bronze tripod overthrown, and the vale of Delphi desolate, still the Pythia is not dead." [5]

Sybil, then, is like the song of pure art, and to marry her is to enter a sparkling world of romance, entirely beautiful and untainted:

> Never for a single moment did Lord Arthur regret all that he had suffered for Sybil's sake, while she, on her side, gave him the best things a woman can give to any man—worship, tenderness, and love. For them romance was not killed by reality. They always felt young. ["Crime," p. 59]

This is pure fairy tale, the world that Rossetti sought and never found, the world that Poe longed for and could have reached in the symbolic Lenore. Lord Arthur attains it. It is the higher innocence, which can be attained only after the child's world of innocence has been destroyed and the problem of evil faced and solved.

"The Fisherman and His Soul" is one of Wilde's later fairy tales. It again deals with the fall from the world of innocence and the attainment of a higher innocence, but it counterpoints "Lord Arthur Savile's Crime" in its treatment of the demonic. Lord Arthur reaches a state of higher innocence by destroying Podgers, but the young fisherman attains it only after his heart grows large enough to include in love both the beautiful

5. Oscar Wilde, *Miscellanies*, ed. Robert Ross, p. 114. All future references to Wilde's miscellanies are to this edition and are cited in parentheses in the text. The edition will be designated as *Miscellanies*.

mermaid and his evil soul. The story is a humorless and puzzling one, but is worthy of detailed analysis because it shows the development of Wilde's attitude toward the demonic in the fairy tales and also reveals how extremely symbolic he could be in his thinking.

Essentially, we have two worlds in "The Fisherman and His Soul": the beautiful underwater world of the mermaid and the demonic world of dry land, a world of evil and suffering. This split is indicated at the very opening of the story:

> Every morning the young Fisherman went out upon the sea, and threw his nets into the water.
>
> When the wind blew from the land he caught nothing, or but little at best, for it was a bitter and black-winged wind, and rough waves rose up to meet it. But when the wind blew to the shore, the fish came in from the deep, and swam into the meshes of his nets, and he took them to the market-place and sold them.[6]

The fisherman belongs on dry land, but he is drawn to the sea, as his occupation clearly indicates. The two worlds are separate and apparently irreconcilable, however. When the fisherman catches a stunningly beautiful mermaid in his net, he finds that he cannot marry her:

> And one evening he called to her and said: "Little Mermaid, little Mermaid, I love thee. Take me for thy bridegroom, for I love thee."
>
> But the Mermaid shook her head. "Thou hast a human

6. Oscar Wilde, *A House of Pomegranates and Other Tales,* ed. Robert Ross, p. 67. All future references to the fairy tales contained here are to this edition and are cited in parentheses in the text. The edition will be designated as *Pomegranates* except when the reference is to a tale from the *Happy Prince* collection. Then the edition will be designated as *Prince.* Wilde brought out two collections of fairy tales—*The Happy Prince and Other Tales* and, later on, the collection *A House of Pomegranates.* Robert Ross has placed the two in one volume under the title of the second collection, but it is important for my purposes to distinguish between these two collections in the text.

soul," she answered. "If only thou wouldst send away thy
soul, then could I love thee." [*Pomegranates*, p. 72]

The mermaid is a concentrated symbol of the beautiful,
dazzling undersea world, and she refuses to come into contact
with anything that is ugly or that belongs to the demonic dry
land. She is not human, however. She helps the fisherman only
in his capacity as fisherman, and is willing to love him only if
he abandons the human part of himself, his soul, for "the
Sea-folk have no souls." The fisherman, being young, exists in
a boyish, carefree world of innocence, is insulated from any
knowledge of evil, and yearns to unite only with what is beautiful. "Of what use is my soul to me?" he asks himself. "I cannot see it. I may not touch it. I do not know it. Surely I will
send it away from me, and much gladness shall be mine"
(*Pomegranates*, p. 72).

In order to get rid of his soul, the fisherman first goes to a
priest, but the priest informs him that the soul is infinitely
valuable and curses the sea-folk as soulless. The merchants, on
the other hand, refuse to buy his soul because it has no value
whatsoever. He finally goes to a red-haired witch, who takes
him to a Witches' Sabbath and introduces him to a proud,
well-dressed gentleman, the Devil himself. It is a measure of
the young fisherman's innocence at this point that he does
not realize the danger he is in. Nor does he recognize the well-
dressed gentleman. The Devil exudes such an aura of evil,
though, that the fisherman, on approaching him, involuntarily
makes the sign of the cross and calls on God's name. The
witches shriek and fly away, and the Devil sadly withdraws,
but the fisherman captures the red-haired witch and forces her
to tell him how to cast off his soul.

It is the fisherman's heart, not his soul, that occupies the
position of highest importance in this tale, for love is seen as
the supreme value and the road to salvation. The soul's problem is that the fisherman's love is exclusive—his heart belongs
to the mermaid alone. Consequently, the soul is cast off without a heart:

And his Soul said to him, "If indeed thou must drive
me from thee, send me not forth without a heart. The
world is cruel, give me thy heart to take with me."
He tossed his head and smiled. "With what should I
love my love if I gave thee my heart?" he cried.
"Nay, but be merciful," said his Soul: "Give me thy
heart, for the world is very cruel, and I am afraid."
"My heart is my love's," he answered, "therefore tarry
not, but get thee gone."
"Should I not love also?" asked his Soul.
"Get thee gone, for I have no need of thee," cried the
young Fisherman. [*Pomegranates*, pp. 87–88]

Exiled to the demon universe of dry land, the soul, cast off
without a heart, becomes thoroughly evil. The fisherman, on
the other hand, is now able to reject the dry land completely
and live in an underwater world of innocence with the mermaid. The fisherman opens his heart only to the beautiful
mermaid and allows the mermaid to occupy it. The mermaid
unites with the fisherman—"nor shall our lives be divided"—
and dwells within his heart while the soul is banished alto-
gether from his body.

The fisherman's state of innocence cannot last forever,
though, which is indicated by the fact that he obviously cannot consummate his relationship with the mermaid. The
fisherman's world of innocence, moreover, exists through an
unnatural fragmentation, a destruction of the unity of body
and soul that renders the fisherman inhuman. The soul car-
ries the full burden of this fragmentation, and it yearns to re-
unite with its body. The soul now exists as the opposite of the
mermaid, a concentrated symbol of the evil and suffering that
constitute the dry land. Once each year it tempts the fisherman to take it back. The first year it tempts him with a lying
offer of total wisdom:

"Do but suffer me to enter into thee again and be thy
servant, and thou shalt be wiser than all the wise men,

and Wisdom shall be thine. Suffer me to enter into thee, and none will be as wise as thou."

But the young Fisherman laughed. "Love is better than Wisdom," he cried, "and the little Mermaid loves me."

"Nay, but there is nothing better than Wisdom," said the Soul.

"Love is better," answered the young Fisherman, and he plunged into the deep, and the Soul went weeping away over the marshes. [*Pomegranates,* p. 99]

The second year, the evil soul tempts the fisherman with a lying offer of great wealth, but he again rejects the offer in favor of love. The third year, however, the soul tempts the fisherman with a more beautiful lover than the mermaid:

"Her face was veiled with a veil of gauze, but her feet were naked. Naked were her feet, and they moved over the carpet like little white pigeons. Never have I seen anything so marvellous, and the city in which she dances is but a day's journey from this place."

Now when the young Fisherman heard the words of his Soul, he remembered that the little Mermaid had no feet and could not dance. And a great desire came over him, and he said to himself, "It is but a day's journey, and I can return to my love," and he laughed, and stood up in the shallow water, and strode towards the shore. [*Pomegranates,* p. 111]

The fisherman's motive for leaving the mermaid is a deep love for what is beautiful. Also, the fisherman is coming of age—he now wants a human lover, not one whose lower half is a fish's tail. The new lover's face is veiled, and it is her lower limbs that attract him. There is little beauty on the dry land, however, as he finds when he takes his soul back. The soul leads the fisherman to commit acts of evil, but the fisherman soon rebels and tries to cast out his soul again. He discovers that the act can only be performed once. Symbolically,

what this means is that the world of innocence, once abandoned, can never be re-entered.

Evil is no longer an external and banished part of the fisherman, it is now a vital part of his nature, one he is intensely
aware of, and he must either deal with it effectively or remain
forever trapped in the demon universe into which he has
stepped. The fisherman refuses to remain in the demon universe, so he returns to the seashore and calls to his beloved
mermaid. But the mermaid does not answer, nor can he
plunge beneath the waves to seek her anymore—the undersea
world is closed to him. For three years he remains by the seashore, motivated by the power of love, calling to the mermaid
every morning, noon, and evening.

The soul, wishing the fisherman to return to the dry land,
tempts him first with evil, hoping to destroy the love in his
heart:

> And ever did his Soul tempt him with evil, and whisper
> of terrible things. Yet did it not prevail against him, so
> great was the power of his love. [*Pomegranates*, p. 121]

Then it tempts him with good:

> So he spake to the young Fisherman and said, "I have
> told thee of the joy of the world, and thou hast turned a
> deaf ear to me. Suffer me now to tell thee of the world's
> pain, and it may be that thou wilt hearken. . . . To and
> fro over the fens go the lepers, and they are cruel to each
> other. The beggars go up and down on the highways, and
> their wallets are empty. Through the streets of the cities
> walks Famine, and the Plague sits at their gates. Come,
> let us go forth and mend these things, and make them not
> to be. Wherefore shouldst thou tarry here calling to thy
> love, seeing she comes not to thy call? And what is love,
> that thou shouldst set this high store upon it?"
> But the young Fisherman answered it not, so great was
> the power of his love. [*Pomegranates*, p. 122]

Finally the soul despairs, yields to the power of love, and asks
to be purified—a request it would never have made had it
been sold to the Devil:

> "Lo! now I have tempted thee with evil, and I have
> tempted thee with good, and thy love is stronger than I
> am. Wherefore will I tempt thee no longer, but I pray
> thee to suffer me to enter thy heart, that I may be one
> with thee even as before."
> "Surely thou mayest enter," said the young Fisherman,
> "for in the days when with no heart thou didst go
> through the world thou must have much suffered."
> "Alas!" cried his Soul, "I can find no place of entrance,
> so compassed about with love is this heart of thine."
> "Yet I would that I could help thee," said the young
> Fisherman. [*Pomegranates*, p. 123]

The fisherman is now ready to attain a state of higher innocence. His desire to help and love his demonic soul is a genuine one, and it deals a final blow to the beautiful, exclusive
world of innocence:

> And as he spake there came a great cry of mourning
> from the sea, even the cry that men hear when one of the
> Sea-folk is dead. And the young Fisherman leapt up, and
> left his wattled house, and ran down to the shore. And
> the black waves came hurrying to the shore, bearing with
> them a burden that was whiter than silver. White as the
> surf it was, and like a flower it tossed on the waves. And
> the surf took it from the waves, and the foam took it
> from the surf, and the shore received it, and lying at his
> feet the young Fisherman saw the body of the little Mer-
> maid. Dead at his feet it was lying. [*Pomegranates*, pp.
> 123–24]

The mermaid exists within the fisherman's heart as something
very beautiful and fragile, something that cannot come into
contact with evil and survive. As soon as the fisherman begins
to open his heart to his soul, the mermaid dies.

The late nineteenth century was fascinated with the Jekyll-Hyde character. In "Lord Arthur Savile's Crime," Sybil and Podgers are projections of the Jekyll-Hyde split within the protagonist. In "The Fisherman and His Soul," the mermaid and the soul are the same projections. Sybil, unlike the mermaid, suggests a higher innocence distinct from Arthur's initial world of careless, boyish insouciance, but both Podgers and the soul embody the demonic, which is at once inside and outside the protagonist. Arthur attains a state of higher innocence by destroying Podgers and loving and marrying Sybil. For the fisherman, the road is a very different one indeed:

> The black sea came nearer, and the white foam moaned like a leper. With white claws of foam the sea grabbed at the shore. . . .
> And his Soul besought him to depart, but he would not, so great was his love. And the sea came nearer, and sought to cover him with its waves, and when he knew that the end was at hand he kissed with mad lips the cold lips of the Mermaid, and the heart that was within him brake. And as through the fulness of his love his heart did break, the Soul found an entrance and entered in, and was one with him even as before. And the sea covered the young Fisherman with its waves. [*Pomegranates,* pp. 125–26]

The fisherman dies, but he has attained a state of higher innocence and his place is now in heaven. His heart embraces in love both the mermaid and the soul at exactly the same time that distinctions between sea and dry land are swept away. By following the road of love, he finally manages to put an end to fragmentation within a framework of total purity. The mermaid acquires a soul—the fisherman's—the soul acquires a heart and is purified, and the fisherman reconciles the warring aspects of himself. The initial world of innocence was one of love, but a private, exclusive love limited to the beautiful mermaid. The higher innocence is again a world of love, but one that is all-encompassing. It is the lesson of total love that the priest learns in the end, as flowers burst from the barren soil over the fisherman's grave. He had earlier cursed the dead fisherman, the mermaid, the sea, and the sea-folk as godless, and had ordered the fisherman and the mermaid to be buried in barren ground. The grave blooms, however, and the flowers cause a strange transformation in the priest. The tale ends with the priest preaching God's love and blessing all of God's creatures and works:

> And in the morning, while it was still dawn, he went forth with the monks and the musicians, and the candle-bearers and the swingers of censers, and a great company, and came to the shore of the sea, and [blessed] all the wild things that are in it. The Fauns also he blessed, and the little things that dance in the woodland, and the bright-eyed things that peer through the leaves. All the things in God's world he blessed, and the people were filled with joy and wonder. [*Pomegranates*, pp. 128–29]

No one and nothing is excluded.

This fall from the world of innocence and subsequent attainment of a higher innocence is the governing principle of Wilde's fairy tales. Not all the tales reproduce this pattern in its entirety: some begin with the higher innocence, such as "The Nightingale and the Rose"; some never go beyond the child's world of innocence, as for example "The Birthday of the Infanta"; but the pulsing heart of the fairy tales, the thread that runs through all of them and ties them together, is this theme of the fall and the discovery of a higher innocence.

In brief, the world of innocence is a beautiful world that is blissfully unaware of the other, demonic side of existence. The demonic side of life is a universe of suffering or evil or both, and it may be internal, external, or both. The child begins in the world of innocence, but the process of maturing inevitably shatters this world and forces him to confront the demonic in

life. The third stage, as in Blake, is the attainment of a higher
innocence. This is total spiritual purity, and the road to it is
love. It can only be reached after the world of innocence has
been destroyed and the demon universe faced and dealt with
effectively.

"The Canterville Ghost"—perhaps Wilde's most famous
fairy tale—is somewhat marred because of its unfortunate attempt to reproduce this entire pattern. The story begins in
the world of innocence, and here Wilde is brilliant. Practically
every British child knows the story of the American family
that rented a haunted castle in England, refused at first to believe that it was haunted, then tried to chase the ghost away
with pesticides, and finally laughed it into a nervous break-
down.

There is a serious point to all this, though. The ghost is
evil—it recalls its past crimes with glee—but the innocent
American family refuses to recognize the demonic or to treat
it seriously. Virginia, however, a virgin who is just coming of
age, finally take pity on the neurotic ghost and agrees to help
it die. As a result, she opens herself to the full experience of
the demonic, disappears into a vast dark hole, and emerges a
while later with a box of indescribably valuable jewels given
to her by the grateful ghost.

The jewels symbolize Virginia's attainment of a higher innocence. Her ability to love and pity the ghost has led to her
total purification. She has developed a heart large enough to
include everyone—even the British aristocracy, which her re-
publican father continues to attack until the end. Unfortunately, however, the world of innocence Wilde portrays is
so delightful that the story does not survive its loss. Virginia's
development beyond this world is pale and uninteresting.

"The Happy Prince" also reproduces the entire fairy-tale
pattern. The prince begins as a blissful boy who, after his
death, becomes a beautiful statue high above the city and is
happy because of his beauty. His cocoonlike world of beauty
is soon shattered, however, for he realizes that a great deal of
suffering exists in the city. Bit by bit, he strips himself of his

beautiful jewels and gold leaf and gives them to the poor. Finally all his beauty is gone, and his lead heart breaks when the swallow who had been helping him dies, after undergoing a similar pattern of development. The story ends thus:

> "Bring me the two most precious things in the city," said God to one of His angels; and the angel brought Him the leaden heart and the dead bird.
>
> "You have rightly chosen," said God, "for in my garden of Paradise this little bird shall sing for evermore, and in my city of gold the Happy Prince shall praise me." [*Prince*, p. 183]

The higher innocence—far more beautiful than the first world of innocence—has been reached. Totally pure, their hearts overflowing with love, the prince and the swallow enter heaven forever.

"The Selfish Giant" is another variation on the same theme. The giant's castle and garden are beautiful, but he selfishly excludes a group of children from the garden and builds a wall to keep them out. The children suffer, but the giant does not care. The giant, having become aware of human suffering and refusing to feel love and pity, finds his beautiful private world shattered. A perpetual winter—the symbol of his fallen nature—descends upon his castle and garden, until the children manage to creep back in through a crack in the wall. They bring the spring with them, and the giant rushes out to meet them. They all run away, however, except for one tiny child whose eyes are so full of tears that he does not see the giant coming. "And the Giant's heart melted" at the child's suffering; he helps him, then knocks the wall down. The children, seeing that the giant has changed, return to the garden and come there daily after that. When the giant is old and ready to die, Christ personally comes and takes him to heaven, appearing in the form of the child the giant had helped many years before. But the giant, of course, had really entered heaven many years earlier, when his heart melted for the little child.

"The Young King" again reproduces the entire pattern of

the fall from innocence and the achievement of a higher innocence. It is a story worthy of special notice, however, because
the Christian ethos of the fairy tales is at its most intense
here, and because "The Young King" will later prove helpful
in understanding *De Profundis*. The tale begins with the cruel
murder of a pure white princess and a beautiful aesthetic
artist by order of the diabolical old king. The princess and the
artist had married in secret. Their newly born son, the young
king, is disowned and given to a goatherd to be raised. Realizing on his deathbed that he has no heir, however, the old king
sends for his disowned grandson and names him as the heir.
"From the first moment of his recognition," Wilde tells us, the
young king "had shown signs of that strange passion for beauty
that was destined to have so great an influence over his life"
(*Pomegranates*, p. 5). The son of aesthetes, he reacts aesthet-
ically to his surroundings:

> The wonderful palace—*Joyeuse,* as they called it—of
> which he now found himself lord, seemed to him to be a
> new world fresh-fashioned for his delight; and as soon as
> he could escape from the council-board or audience-cham-
> ber, he would run down the great staircase with its lions
> of gilt bronze and its steps of bright porphyry, and wan-
> der from room to room, and from corridor to corridor,
> like one who was seeking an anodyne from pain, a sort of
> restoration from sickness.
>
> Upon these journeys of discovery, as he would call
> them—and indeed, they were to him real voyages through
> a marvellous land, he would sometimes be accompanied
> by the slim, fair-haired Court pages, with their floating
> mantles, and gay fluttering ribands; but more often he
> would be alone, feeling through a certain quick instinct
> which was almost a divination, that the secrets of art are
> best learned in secret, and that Beauty, like Wisdom,
> loves the lonely worshipper. [*Pomegranates*, p. 6]

I have quoted at length because this is an extremely important passage. The young king's journeys of discovery are
journeys of self-discovery. His nature had been suppressed in

peasant surroundings, but he has now found a new world whose beauty is the external manifestation of the "marvellous land" within. It is the world of his parents, whose nature he has inherited and is now exploring. The young king's world of innocence is not devoid of evil, however. This is symbolized by the fact that, though his parents were a pure white princess and a beautiful foreign artist, the young king's grandfather was the old king. The council-boards and audience-chambers are associated with the old king, and they create in the young king a spiritual pain that can be cured only by the beauty of art. As in "The Palace of Art," however, the young king's art world is private and therefore selfish: he excludes from it even the innocent "slim, fair-haired Court pages."

"The Young King" is about the coming-of-age of the young king. When found, "he was only a lad, being but sixteen years of age" (*Pomegranates*, p. 3). In "Lord Arthur Savile's Crime," marriage symbolizes the transition from boyhood to manhood. Here the symbol is the assumption of the authorities and responsibilities of kingship, and it is on the night before his coronation that the young king fully confronts the demonic element hitherto latent within himself.

Of all the beautiful art objects in the palace, most of them brought there by him, the young king finds his coronation robe of tissued gold, his ruby-studded crown, and his pearl-decorated scepter to be the most artistically pleasing. In three successive dreams, however—the first beginning at midnight— he comes to a vivid realization of the huge amount of evil and suffering that went into the making of the robe and the procuring of the rubies and pearls. Sleep is a state of mind where conscious thoughts are laid to rest and thoughts that lie beneath the surface emerge. The young king is now forced to explore a different aspect of his nature. What he was only subconsciously aware of when he gave the orders to fashion the robe, crown, and scepter, he now becomes terrifyingly aware of:

> Then the diver came up for the last time, and the pearl
> that he brought with him was fairer than all the pearls

of Ormuz, for it was shaped like the full moon, and whiter than the morning star. But his face was strangely pale, and as he fell upon the deck the blood gushed from his ears and nostrils. He quivered a little, and then he was still. The negroes shrugged their shoulders, and threw the body overboard.

And the master of the galley laughed, and, reaching out, he took the pearl, and when he saw it he pressed it to his forehead and bowed. "It shall be," he said, "for the sceptre of the young king." [*Pomegranates*, p. 15]

The result is that guilt destroys the young king's enjoyment of an art world founded on evil and suffering:

"Take these things away, and hide them from me. Though it be the day of my coronation, I will not wear them. For on the loom of Sorrow, and by the white hands of Pain, has this robe been woven. There is Blood in the heart of the ruby, and Death in the heart of the pearl." [*Pomegranates*, p. 20]

The young king's three dreams constitute a fall into the demon universe. His enclosed world of artistic beauty is shattered, and he becomes irreversibly and unbearably aware of the pain of others and his complicity in causing this pain. Instead of accepting his position and becoming a carbon copy of the old king, however, the young king's nature propels him to purge himself of evil and enter a state of complete purity. Christ is the symbol of the higher innocence the young king seeks. Motivated by a deep love for suffering humanity, he dons a beggar's robe and a crown of thorns and goes to his coronation.

His attempt to assume a Christ-like stature, however, is opposed by the realm. The whole kingdom—nobles, workers, clergy—makes a concerted effort to keep the young king in the demon universe. All argue in favor of a fragmented society in which men are not brothers. The last and subtlest argument comes from the bishop, who sincerely contends that evil is an integral part of the world and that man cannot alter this: "In

the salt-marshes live the lepers; they have houses of wattled
reed, and none may come nigh them. The beggars wander
through the cities, and eat their food with the dogs. Canst
thou make these things not to be? Wilt thou take the leper for
thy bedfellow, and set the beggar at thy board? Shall the lion
do thy bidding, and the wild boar obey thee?" (Pomegranates,
p. 25). The young king, however, refuses to be seduced by
this argument and insists on following the path of love to its
ultimate destination. Earlier, in the world of innocence, he
had worshiped a picture from Venice and had spent a whole
night contemplating a statue of Endymion. Now he stands before a different statue:

> He stood before the image of Christ, and on his right
> hand and on his left were the marvellous vessels of gold,
> the chalice with the yellow wine, and the vial with the
> holy oil. He knelt before the image of Christ, and the
> great candles burned brightly by the jewelled shrine, and
> the smoke of the incense curled in thin blue wreaths
> through the dome. [Pomegranates, pp. 25–26]

It should be stressed that Christ is connected with beautiful
art objects. Wilde, in this tale, dissolves all differences between
Christ and the highest manifestation of the artistic impulse,
and identifies Christ with the highest and most beautiful art.
The young king prays, then rises and faces the nobles who
have entered the cathedral to slay him. But a strange thing
happens:

> And lo! through the painted windows came the sun-
> light streaming upon him, and the sun-beams wove round
> him a tissued robe that was fairer than the robe that had
> been fashioned for his pleasure. The dead staff blossomed,
> and bare lilies that were whiter than pearls. The dry
> thorn blossomed, and bare roses that were redder than
> rubies. Whiter than fine pearls were the lilies, and their
> stems were of bright silver. Redder than male rubies were
> the roses, and their leaves were of beaten gold. . . . He

stood there in a king's raiment, and the Glory of God filled the place, and the saints in their carven niches seemed to move. [*Pomegranates*, pp. 26–27]

God, in crowning the young king and elevating him to the stature of Christ, simultaneously creates for him a world of art that is far purer and more beautiful than the old world that had its roots in human suffering. The young king receives a new robe, a new scepter, and a new crown, far superior to the ones he had rejected and refused to wear. These new objects, moreover, are completely pure: they are straight from God and have no connection with human suffering. They are also public, symbols of the new reign that is about to commence, a reign of love and forgiveness for all. The young king, in attaining the higher innocence, becomes a second Christ, reconciles all fragmentation within a framework of love, and simultaneously enters the highest and most beautiful possible world of art.

"The Star-Child" again follows the entire fairy-tale pattern. The star-child begins, quite literally, in a cocoonlike world of beauty—enfolded in "a cloak of golden tissue, curiously wrought with stars, and wrapped in many folds" (*Pomegranates*, p. 136). Although he comes to the world seemingly as a gift from the stars, he is brought up by a woodcutter's family. As he grows physically more beautiful each year, he also becomes proud and disdainful, despising the ugly and the poor and actually inflicting pain upon them. He becomes progressively more evil until he loses his symbolic star-parentage and acquires a new symbolic parent—a ragged, ugly, bleeding beggar-woman, who reveals herself as his mother. Though he rejects her disdainfully, the sparkling world of his star-parents vanishes: he loses his beauty and turns into a scaly monster. When the star-child's world of beauty is shattered, he finds himself a hideous part of the universe of pain and ugliness. After many severe trials and humiliations, he acquires a heart, purges himself of evil, and reaches a state of higher innocence. The symbols of the higher innocence are the regaining of his physical beauty, his new parents—a king and queen—and his new status as king. As an adolescent, he led a group of village boys in evil deeds, but he now leads a kingdom in love. Interestingly, though, the star-child dies within three years, for his sufferings have been too terrible and searing. If one's fall from the world of innocence is not cushioned, it seems, one may remain scarred for life or be utterly destroyed by the demon universe.

The other fairy tales do not fully reproduce a person's fall from the world of innocence and the attainment of a higher innocence, but they are nevertheless governed, in varying degrees, by this pattern. In "The Birthday of the Infanta," for instance, the Infanta remains in the world of innocence from beginning to end, but the tale is a clear appeal to the reader to recognize human suffering, develop a heart, and attain a state of higher innocence. The dwarf whose act amuses the Infanta so much falls in love with her. He stalks into the palace to declare his love, but catches sight of himself in a mirror, recognizes that he is ugly and misshapen, and dies of a broken heart. The Infanta finds the dwarf's inert body and insists that he dance for her once more:

> "Mi bella Princesa, your funny little dwarf will never dance again. It is a pity, for he is so ugly that he might have made the king smile."
>
> "But why will he not dance again?" asked the Infanta, laughing.
>
> "Because his heart is broken," answered the Chamberlain.
>
> And the Infanta frowned, and her dainty rose-leaf lips curled in pretty disdain. "For the future let those who come to play with me have no hearts," she cried, and she ran out into the garden. [Pomegranates, p. 64]

The tale clearly does not endorse the Infanta's heartlessness, but rather appeals to the reader to develop beyond it.

In "The Nightingale and the Rose," we have a student who exists in the fallen world and a nightingale who is al-

ready approaching the highest state of love. The student—
who diligently pursues the disciplines of logic, philosophy,
and metaphysics—is downcast because he cannot find a red
rose for his love. The nightingale tries to find him a rose, but
discovers that the price she must pay for it is her own life.
The rose-tree sadly informs her that "if you want a red rose,
. . . you must build it out of music by moonlight, and stain
it with your own heart's-blood" (*Prince*, p. 191). The nightingale does this:

> The nightingale pressed closer against the thorn, and
> the thorn touched her heart, and a fierce pang of pain
> shot through her. Bitter, bitter was the pain, and wilder
> and wilder grew her song, for she sang of the Love that is
> perfected by Death, of the Love that dies not in the tomb.
> [*Prince*, p. 195]

The nightingale dies, but her love—like Christ's—is "the
Love that dies not in the tomb." And indeed, the thorn does
suggest that the nightingale has attained a Christ-like stature.
The student, on the other hand, is rejected by his love because
the rose does not go with her dress and because he is not rich
enough. Cynically, he tosses the rose away, declares that love
is silly and not half as useful as logic, and returns to his room
to read a dusty book. It turns out that the student is hopelessly
lost in the fallen world and knows nothing of love. Because of
him, however, the nightingale has attained utter spiritual
purity through a self-sacrificial act of love, and she goes, one
assumes, straight to heaven, where she will join the happy
prince and the swallow.

"The Devoted Friend" is about two friends, little Hans and
big Hugh the miller. Big Hugh is entirely selfish and befriends
Hans simply because of what Hans can do for him. Big Hugh
is rich, and he lives with his family in a beautiful home from
which he excludes all that suffers or is ugly. Little Hans, on the
other hand, is poor and "not distinguished at all, except for
his kind heart" (*Prince*, p. 213). Hans, motivated by friendship, continually does favors for big Hugh until the last favor

costs him his life. Because of friendship and love, Hans endangers his life to get a doctor for big Hugh's boy, and he dies in a storm. But Hans's act of love, like that of the nightingale, is really the attainment of complete spiritual purity, and his place is now in heaven.

"The Remarkable Rocket" is an entirely comic study in selfishness. The remarkable rocket is totally self-centered and makes the following statement to the other fireworks: "I am always thinking about myself, and I expect everybody else to do the same. That is what is called sympathy" (*Prince*, p. 242). He outlines his virtues in great detail to the other fireworks, insists that he should be admired, and actually cries in order to prove his sympathetic nature. The rocket's tears so dampen his powder, however, that he fails to go off at the appointed time—the celebration of the prince's wedding—and is therefore discarded and tossed into a mudpile. Finally, two boys use him for firewood and he does go off. The spectacle is quite beautiful, but the remarkable rocket is the only one around to admire it—even the two boys are asleep. Since the rocket is completely selfish, his beautiful world remains private and his need for admiration is frustrated. And his beautiful world is ephemeral: the unseen spectacle soon ends, and the rocket falls back to the earth, a burnt-out stick. The world of innocence cannot last forever, though the rocket, to the end, does not realize that he must develop beyond this world and become truly sympathetic. Consequently, once the world of innocence is shattered, the rocket gasps and dies.

If one reads Wilde's fairy tales in the order of their composition, one notices that the demonic element in them grows steadily more sinister until it threatens to break out of the fairy-tale mold and destroy it. The movement from "Lord Arthur Savile's Crime" through *The Happy Prince and Other Tales* to the tales of *A House of Pomegranates* is toward an increasing awareness of the demonic and a corresponding inability to control and contain it. In the earlier tales, Wilde usually presents the demonic in a light-hearted way. For

example, in "The Selfish Giant," Wilde's presentation of the
demonic is playful:

> The Snow covered up the grass with her great white
> cloak, and the Frost painted all the trees silver. Then
> they invited the North Wind to stay with them, and he
> came. He was wrapped in furs, and he roared all day
> about the garden, and blew the chimney-pots down. "This
> is a delightful spot," he said; "we must ask the Hail on a
> visit." So the Hail came. Every day for three hours he
> rattled on the roof of the castle till he broke most of the
> slates, and then he ran round and round the garden as
> fast as he could go. He was dressed in gray, and his breath
> was like ice. [*Prince*, p. 203]

The late fairy tale, "The Young King," however, uses the
same method of personification to give us a relatively sinister
picture of the demonic:

> And Death laughed again, and he whistled through his
> fingers, and a woman came flying through the air. Plague
> was written upon her forehead, and a crowd of lean
> vultures wheeled round her. She covered the valley with
> her wings, and no man was left alive.
>
> And Avarice fled shrieking through the forest, and
> Death leaped upon his red horse and galloped away, and
> his galloping was faster than the wind.
>
> And out of the slime at the bottom of the valley crept
> dragons and horrible things with scales, and the jackals
> came trotting along the sand, sniffing up the air with their
> nostrils. [*Pomegranates*, pp. 18–19]

Examples of this change in mood abound. In the early "The
Remarkable Rocket," the selfish assertion of superiority is presented in a harmless way:

> "My father was a rocket like myself, and of French ex-
> traction. He flew so high that the people were afraid that
> he would never come down again. He did, though, for he

was of a kindly disposition, and he made a most brilliant descent in a shower of golden rain. The newspapers wrote about his performance in very flattering terms. Indeed, the Court Gazette called him a triumph of Pylotechnic art."

"Pyrotechnic, Pyrotechnic, you mean," said a Bengal Light; "I know it is Pyrotechnic, for I saw it on my own canister."

"Well, I said Pylotechnic," answered the Rocket, in a severe tone of voice, and the Bengal Light felt so crushed that he began at once to bully the little squibs in order to show that he was still a person of some importance. [*Prince*, p. 241]

In the later "The Star-Child," the selfish assertion of superiority is presented differently:

And his companions followed him, for he was fair, and fleet of foot, and could dance, and pipe, and make music. And wherever the Star-Child led them they followed, and whatever the Star-Child bade them do, that did they. And when he pierced with a sharp reed the dim eyes of the mole, they laughed, and when he cast stones at the leper they laughed also. [*Pomegranates*, p. 142]

We have moved from a rocket bullying a Bengal light to a beautiful young boy piercing a harmless animal's eyes with a sharp reed.

Along with the increasingly sinister presentation of the demonic element, the movement of Wilde's fairy tales shows a steady lessening of the comic element. The two trends are inextricable and interdependent. As the demonic element becomes more central and disturbing, it ceases to be funny and can no longer be treated comically. "Lord Arthur Savile's Crime" is comic from beginning to end. Even Arthur's exploration of the fallen world remains comic, for there is no objective correlative between Podgers's reading of Arthur's palm and Arthur's reaction to the reading. The early fairy tale

"The Devoted Friend" is also comic from beginning to end, despite its grim theme of what amounts to the murder of little Hans by big Hugh.

The tales of *The Happy Prince* collection, however—of which "The Devoted Friend" is a part—are not entirely comic. Two of the five tales, "The Devoted Friend" and "The Remarkable Rocket," are comic all the way through, but "The Selfish Giant" is rather touching as the giant attains the higher innocence and is finally claimed by Christ. "The Nightingale and the Rose" mixes the comic and the serious. The nightingale's self-sacrifice is moving, but the student's experience with the girl he thinks he loves is comic—or at any rate has comic elements. "The Happy Prince" is largely serious, except in its amusing presentation of utilitarian attitudes.

The tales of *A House of Pomegranates,* on the other hand, are almost entirely lacking in humor. There is no humor in "The Young King," except for a single joke in the opening paragraph. In "The Birthday of the Infanta," the tone is quite serious, though the Infanta remains in the world of innocence from begining to end. "The Fisherman and His Soul" is not comic. "The Star-Child" begins comically, but that element disappears after the opening paragraphs and never appears again. The movement of Wilde's fairy tales, then, is toward the elimination of the comic element.

In the later fairy tales, moreover, it is not enough to become aware of the demonic element—one must incorporate it within an all-inclusive framework of love. This becomes especially clear when we compare "Lord Arthur Savile's Crime" and "The Fisherman and His Soul." As has already been indicated, in the earlier tale Arthur becomes aware of Podgers but tosses him into the Thames and attains a state of higher innocence by loving and marrying Sybil; he never feels any love or pity for Podgers. In the later tale, however, the fisherman attains the higher innocence only when his heart becomes large enough to include both the beautiful mermaid and his own demonic soul. Podgers and his fallen world are destroyed, but the soul and its evil, agonized world of dry land are loved and purified. These two tales stand at opposite ends of the spectrum, but a movement is discernible in the fairy tales away from Arthur's inability to love and pity the demonic.

The early "The Canterville Ghost"—written very shortly after "Lord Arthur Savile's Crime"—may be seen as transitional in this respect: the ghost, though sent to its grave, is pitied and loved by Virginia. This movement is again inextricable from the growing concern with the demonic in the fairy tales. As the demonic element becomes more sinister and difficult to control, it can no longer be flipped into the Thames or sent to its grave, but has to be dealt with more realistically. When the young king reaches a state of higher innocence, he acquires a Christ-like stature and a heart large enough to embrace an entire realm, and so does the star-child. For the star-child, the higher innocence unites the beauty of the world of innocence with a deep love for all that suffers and is ugly. In the later fairy tales, then, the demonic element becomes more sinister but is still contained within an all-inclusive framework of love.

And these tales are, after all, fairy tales—a genre that admits the demonic only to neutralize and defeat it. In *The Decay of Lying*, written early during the fairy-tale period, Wilde's main thesis is that the imagination gives meaning to the forms and shapes of the outside world. The pure imagination creates a beautiful world and a Romantic literature, while the fallen imagination produces a Darwinian universe and Zola-like, naturalistic literature.[7] Wilde playfully uses the vocabulary of the fallen imagination throughout the essay, referring to the fallen universe as real, factual, scientific, and to the pure universe as unreal, a dream, a lie. Wilde's view of art at this stage is compactly stated by his character, Vivian:

> *Vivian* (reading). "Art begins with decoration, with
> purely imaginative and pleasurable work dealing with
> what is unreal and non-existent. This is the first stage.

---

7. In *The Critic as Artist*, Wilde projects this idea into the realm of art and argues, not without irony, that the best critic's imagination in effect re-creates the work of art.

Then Life becomes fascinated with this new wonder, and asks to be admitted into the charmed circle. Art takes life as part of her rough material, recreates it, and refashions it in fresh forms, is absolutely indifferent to fact, invents, imagines, dreams, and keeps between herself and reality the impenetrable barrier of beautiful style, of decorative or ideal treatment. The third stage is when Life gets the upper hand, and drives Art out into the wilderness. This is the true decadence, and it is from this that we are now suffering." [8]

The fairy tales belong to the second stage. They admit Life —that is, the fallen world—into their charmed circle, but they refashion and recreate it and never allow it to get the upper hand. They are an assertion of childlike purity. As Wilde wrote of *The Happy Prince and Other Tales* in 1888: "They are studies in prose, put for Romance's sake into a fanciful form: meant partly for children, and partly for those who have kept the child-like faculties of wonder and joy, and who find in simplicity a subtle strangeness." [9] In this respect, the fairy tales are very much like Blake's *Songs of Innocence,* and may be read as Wilde's *Songs of Innocence.* Meant to capture a childlike state of the mind, they are for those who have not yet crossed the threshold from innocence into experience. Their great paradox is that, though their genre places them firmly in the world of innocence, their main theme is the fall from innocence and the attainment of a higher innocence. What Wilde seems to be saying is that one can become aware of the stages beyond innocence without actually being claimed by them—can absorb, as it were, the entire Blakean pattern and contain it within the realm of childlike innocence.

A biographer might read the fairy tales as Wilde's attempt

8. Oscar Wilde, *Intentions and the Soul of Man,* ed. Robert Ross, p. 22. All future references to *Intentions and the Soul of Man* are to this edition and are cited in parentheses in the text. The edition will be designated as *Intentions.*

9. Oscar Wilde, *The Letters of Oscar Wilde,* ed. Rupert Hart-Davis, p. 219. All future references to Wilde's letters are to this edition and are cited in parentheses in the text. The edition will be designated as *Letters.*

to assert the primacy of his family life and to reject the siren call of homosexuality. "Lord Arthur Savile's Crime" revolves around a marriage that cannot succeed until the coarse Podgers—Robert Ross?—is destroyed within the self. As for the other tales, they are probably Wilde's attempt to remain within the charmed circle of his children, innocent and safe from evil. Cyril and Vyvyan, Wilde's two boys, were very young during this period, and Wilde was very attached to both of them—especially Cyril. As the fairy tales insist, however—both in their theme and in their progressively darker vision of the demonic—the movement from innocence to experience is inevitable and must be made.

In *The Picture of Dorian Gray,* Wilde crosses the threshold. Some years later, in 1892, he wrote to Coulson Kernahan, who had sent him a fairy tale, "The Garden of God": "Your strength lies not in such fanciful, winsome work. You must deal directly with Life—modern terrible Life—wrestle with it, and force it to yield you its secret. You have the power and the pen. You know what passion is, what passions are; you can give them their red raiment, and make them move before us. You can fashion puppets with bodies of flesh, and souls of turmoil: and so, you must sit down, and do a great thing" (*Letters,* p. 315).

2 The Darkening Lens

> For a few seconds he stood bending over the balustrade, and peering down into the black seething well of darkness.
>
> WILDE, *The Picture of Dorian Gray*

It is doubtful that *The Picture of Dorian Gray* is "a great thing," but it has survived the test of time and is a deeper and more thoughtful novel than its critics have so far been willing to concede. The book is a strange one, a partly supernatural tale in which the characters are not individuals but symbols that move in a shadowy world of wit and terror. The novel is chiefly a study of various Victorian art movements corresponding to different stages in the development of Victorian human nature, and the main characters are meant to be personifications of these art movements and psychological states. Of central importance is the new art movement and type of person that was emerging in fin-de-siècle England. Dorian, as he degenerates, becomes a perfect example of the decadent, and his picture, as it grows more and more evil, a perfect type of decadent art.

The main difference between a morally committed aesthete and a decadent is that the latter, looking within and discovering not only purity but evil and corruption, yields to the corrupt impulse and tries to find joy and beauty in evil. Finally, the vision of evil becomes unbearable, the decadent has burned all his bridges, and he finds himself trapped in a dark underworld from which he cannot escape.

Lord Arthur Savile is an excellent example of the moral aesthete. Looking within, Arthur discovers not only the pure "Sybil" but also the corrupt and evil "Podgers." He rejects Podgers, however, and does everything in his power to marry

Sybil. Finally, he is led by Providence to destroy Podgers and marry his love, thereby attaining a state of total purity.

The Picture of Dorian Gray is essentially a reversal of the situation in "Lord Arthur Savile's Crime." Sybil and Wotton represent the two opposing forces within Dorian, but Dorian, as soon as he becomes aware of the evil within himself, sells his soul in a fit of rebellion against the laws of God and nature. The determinism of *Dorian Gray*, moreover, contrasts with that of "Lord Arthur Savile's Crime." The idea of an external determining force is here abandoned in favor of a determinism whose springs well up from within the self:

> There are moments, psychologists tell us, when the passion for sin, or what the world calls sin, so dominates a nature, that every fibre of the body, as every cell of the brain, seems to be instinct with fearful impulses. Men and women at such moments lose the freedom of their will. They move to their terrible end as automatons move. Choice is taken from them, and conscience is either killed, or, if it lives at all, lives but to give rebellion its fascination, and disobedience its charm. For all sins, as theologians weary not of reminding us, are sins of disobedience. When that high spirit, that morning-star of evil, fell from heaven, it was as a rebel that he fell.
>
> Callous, concentrated on evil, with stained mind and soul hungry for rebellion, Dorian Gray hastened on, quickening his steps as he went.[1]

A supernatural force does exist in the novel—it grants Dorian's demonic prayer—but that is its sole function. As it turns out, the devil Dorian sells his soul to is Lord Henry Wotton, who exists not only as something external to Dorian but also as a voice within him. *The Picture of Dorian Gray* is a psychological study of a nature—and an art movement—dominated by a passion for sin.

1. Oscar Wilde, *The Picture of Dorian Gray*, ed. Robert Ross, pp. 306–07. All future references to *The Picture of Dorian Gray* are to this edition and are cited in parentheses in the text. The edition will be designated as *Gray*.

If we accept that Dorian died in 1890, the year in which *Dorian Gray* was mostly written and the earlier version published in *Lippincott's Magazine,* then the novel opens in the year 1873. We first meet Dorian shortly after he has passed the age of twenty, and he dies a few months after his thirty-eighth birthday, which he marks by murdering Basil. The novel thus traces Dorian's development over the span of approximately eighteen years, though Wilde's treatment of the passage of time in the novel is highly inadequate and is, perhaps, the book's most serious weak point.

The year 1873 was an important one for Oscar Wilde, for in that year Walter Pater published his *Studies in the History of the Renaissance.* Wilde is reported to have proclaimed during his first meeting with Yeats that *The Renaissance* "is my golden book; I never travel anywhere without it." [2] Much later, in *De Profundis,* he broodingly referred to it as "that book which has had such a strange influence over my life" (*Letters,* p. 471). Indeed, *The Renaissance* casts a long, sinister shadow across *The Picture of Dorian Gray,* and the entire novel seems to be structured with Pater's book as its focal point.

The Picture of Dorian Gray begins in Basil Hallward's studio, with a conversation between Basil and Lord Henry Wotton. These are the two artists in the novel, Basil's art being his painting while Wotton's is his conversation. The two men are opposites: Basil is a largely pure man who yields to a streak of evil in his soul, while Wotton is a highly corrupt man who never commits an immoral action. Basil's attachment to Dorian has a homosexual dimension, and his disappearances are probably for the sake of homosexual relief. (This is clear in the earlier, shorter version of the novel, but Wilde toned it down considerably in the later version.) As for Wotton, Basil says to him: "You are an extraordinary fellow. You never say a moral thing, and you never do a wrong thing" (*Gray,* p. 7). Basil's purity is balanced against Wotton's corruption, while

2. W. B. Yeats, *The Autobiography of William Butler Yeats* (New York: Macmillan, 1953), p. 80.

Basil's wrong actions stand opposed to Wotton's entirely moral existence.

Basil paints Dorian while Dorian is still in a state of innocence. "He seems to me little more than a lad, though he is really over twenty" (*Gray*, p. 16), Basil says; and Wotton, when he first sets eyes on Dorian, corroborates this view: "Lord Henry looked at him. . . . There was something in his face that made him trust him at once. All the candour of youth was there, as well as all youth's passionate purity. One felt that he had kept himself unspotted from the world" (*Gray*, pp. 24–25). The painting is Basil's masterpiece because Dorian is the flawless manifestation of Basil's lost innocence. It is not until Dorian begins to respond to Wotton's poisonous sermon, however, that the picture becomes complete, for the faint flush of evil that comes across Dorian's face renders him the perfect embodiment of the painter's soul, and allows Basil to introduce the finishing touch to his masterpiece.

As I have said, the chief characters in *The Picture of Dorian Gray* are both human types and representatives of different art movements. This is clearest in Dorian, who exists both as a picture and as a human. This neat split allows us to separate decadence as an art movement from decadence as a mode of life, and to examine the two separately. Wilde clouds the issue, however, by making Wotton fasten on the live Dorian and, paradoxically, treat the breathing human being as a work of art. Basil expounds a theory of art straight out of Pater's essay on Leonardo in *The Renaissance*. The artist, Basil argues, searches in the outside world for the perfect manifestation of his own soul. When he finds this object, he can create masterpieces by painting it. Moreover, the proximity of this object can inspire the artist to trace his own soul in the forms of nature. Wotton muses on this theory, then reverses it by deciding to recreate Dorian the human until he becomes a perfect external manifestation of Wotton's own soul:

> He was a marvellous type, too, this lad, whom by so curious a chance he had met in Basil's studio, or could be

fashioned into a marvellous type, at any rate. Grace was
his, and the white purity of boyhood, and beauty such as
old Greek marbles kept for us. There was nothing one
could not do with him. He could be made a Titan or a
toy.

.   .   .   .

Yes; he would try to be to Dorian Gray what, without
knowing it, the lad had been to the painter who had
fashioned the wonderful portrait. He would seek to domi-
nate him—had already, indeed, done so. He would make
that wonderful spirit his own. [*Gray*, pp. 57–58]

That Wotton regards Dorian as an instrument for his art is
clear from the way he thinks about him. In the above quotation, he seems to regard himself as a sculptor and Dorian's
placid Greek soul as his clay. Here is another example of Wotton's thinking about Dorian: "Talking to him was like playing upon an exquisite violin. He answered to every touch and
thrill of the bow" (*Gray*, p. 57).

The process of recreating Dorian begins in Basil's studio,
when Wotton preaches an invidious sermon based heavily on
the Conclusion of Pater's *Renaissance*. There is an important
difference between Pater and Wotton, however. Wotton, by
substituting the word *sensations* for the word *impressions*,
slightly but significantly modifies Pater's doctrine. Pater had
written: "With this sense of the splendour of our experience
and of its awful brevity, gathering all we are into one des-
perate effort to see and touch, we shall hardly have time to
make theories about the things we see and touch. What we
have to do is to be for ever curiously testing new opinions and
courting new impressions." [3] Wotton, on the other hand,
preaches to Dorian: "Live! Live the wonderful life that is in

3. Walter Pater, *The Renaissance: Studies in Art and Poetry*, standard
edition (London: Macmillan, 1907), p. 237. All future references to *The
Renaissance* are to this edition and are cited in parentheses in the text.
The edition will be designated as *Renaissance*. The book first appeared
in 1873 as *Studies in the History of the Renaissance*, but in future editions Pater altered the title.

you! Let nothing be lost upon you. Be always searching for new sensations" (*Gray*, p. 35).

The Conclusion to Pater's *Renaissance* was widely misinterpreted by the young men of his day, who understood it as a call to live a life of indiscriminate sensations—a fact that led Pater to suppress the Conclusion in the second edition of his book. Wilde was too intelligent to have misunderstood Pater's concluding chapter, but it was precisely this Conclusion that sparked the decadent movement in England. And since *The Picture of Dorian Gray* is primarily an examination of the decadent movement, it is proper that Wotton should present Pater's doctrine as it was understood by the decadents, not as Pater meant it to be understood.

There is more to the matter than that, however. In the third edition of *The Renaissance* (1888), Pater restored his Conclusion, but made "some slight changes which bring it closer to my original meaning." [4] The changes are really insignificant, but it is possible, even probable, that Wilde also believed Pater's original meaning needed to be clearly brought out through some "slight changes." The modifications Wotton makes in Pater's Conclusion can therefore be seen as bringing it closer to what Wilde felt was Pater's original meaning. Wotton would then suggest—as Richard Ellmann believes—Walter Pater himself, but Pater as Wilde understood him. "In *The Picture of Dorian Gray*," Ellmann tells us, "Pater is enclosed (like an unhappy dryad caught in a tree trunk) in Lord Henry Wotton. Lord Henry's chief sin is quoting without acknowledgment from the *Renaissance*. . . . Pater, who wrote a review of [*Dorian Gray*], was at great pains to distinguish Lord

4. Ibid., p. 233, n. 1. The entire note reads as follows: "This brief 'Conclusion' was omitted in the second edition of this book, as I conceived it might possibly mislead some of those young men into whose hands it might fall. On the whole, I have thought it best to reprint it here, with some slight changes which bring it closer to my original meaning. I have dealt more fully in *Marius the Epicurean* with the thoughts suggested in it." For a discussion of the changes Pater made in his Conclusion, see A. C. Benson, *Walter Pater* (London: Macmillan, 1911), p. 46.

Henry's philosophy from his own. Wilde seems to have intended not to distinguish them, however, and to offer (through the disastrous effects of Lord Henry's influence upon Dorian) a criticism of Pater." [5]

Wotton's demonic sermon destroys Dorian's state of innocence and plunges him into a state of experience. Paradoxically, Basil has already paved the way for Wotton by excessively worshiping Dorian's physical beauty and making Dorian aware of this beauty. The sermon begs the evil in Dorian to blossom forth, and he responds splendidly:

> He was dimly conscious that entirely fresh influences were at work within him. Yet they seemed to have come really from himself. The few words that Basil's friend had said to him—words spoken by chance, no doubt, and with wilful paradox in them—had touched some secret chord that had never been touched before, but that he felt was now vibrating and throbbing to curious pulses.
>
> Music had stirred him like that. Music had troubled him many times. But music was not articulate. It was not a new world, but rather another chaos, that it created in us. Mere words! How terrible they were! How clear, and vivid, and cruel! One could not escape from them. And yet what a subtle magic there was in them! They seemed to be able to give a plastic form to formless things, and to have a music of their own as sweet as that of viol or of lute. [*Gray*, pp. 29–30]

Wotton's words are associated with music, which is an art. Basil is an artist who uses a brush, but Wotton is an artist who uses words. He is the decadent artist, who will recreate

---

5. Richard Ellmann, "Overtures to *Salome*," in *Oscar Wilde: A Collection of Critical Essays*, ed. Richard Ellmann, p. 88. Like Wotton, moreover, Pater was a paradoxist of sorts, for his Conclusion—as the decadents understood it—ran counter to everything the Victorians held sacred. Ellmann goes considerably further than this in "Overtures to *Salome*," arguing that *The Renaissance* consciously counterpoints *The Stones of Venice* and "is Ruskin inverted."

his evil soul in Dorian and derive pleasure from contemplating his demonic creation.

Wotton's words, however, seem to Dorian to come from within himself, for Wotton as artist is the external manifestation of the evil in Dorian. In Oscar Wilde's works, the movement of negative capability is often reversed, so that the main character seems to absorb the others into himself. Dorian, under the influence of Wotton's sermon, immediately sells his soul to the devil. Symbolically, what this means is that Dorian cannot and never will be able to resist the evil within himself —that is, the voice of Wotton. His passion for sin will be the governing principle of his life.

In his new thirst for sensations, Dorian's first action is to fall in love with Sybil Vane. The development of the decadent is a gradual process, and Dorian, newly emerged from a state of innocence, at first seeks pure sensations remote from evil. It is clear, though, that his love for Sybil Vane—in contrast to Lord Arthur's love for his Sybil—is Dorian's first decadent act. He says to Wotton:

> "It would never have happened if I had not met you. You filled me with a wild desire to know everything about life. For days after I met you, something seemed to throb in my veins. As I lounged in the Park, or strolled down Piccadilly, I used to look at everyone who passed me, and wonder, with a mad curiosity, what sort of lives they led. Some of them fascinated me. Others filled me with terror. There was an exquisite poison in the air. I had a passion for sensations." [*Gray*, p. 76]

Dorian spiritualizes his attachment to Sybil and deceives himself about its highly sensual nature, but Wotton is very aware that the attachment is Dorian's first step in his development as a decadent. This is Wotton's reaction as Dorian raves about Sybil's purity and divinity:

> Lord Henry watched him with a subtle sense of pleasure. How different he was now from the shy, frightened

boy he had met in Basil Hallward's studio! His nature had
blossomed like a flower, had borne blossoms of scarlet
flame. Out of its secret hiding-place had crept his Soul,
and Desire had come to meet it on the way. [*Gray*, p. 87]

Sybil is a character who knows nothing of evil. Unlike her
counterpart in "Lord Arthur Savile's Crime," however, she
exists in a childlike world of innocence, and it is stressed over
and over again that she is still immature. "There is something
of a child about her," says Dorian, and goes on to say that
when they first met they "stood looking at each other like
children" (*Gray*, p. 85). Sybil, moreover, is presented not as an
individual but as the embodiment of a state of the soul and
an entire movement in Victorian art. Pater, in *The Renaissance*, wrote of the Mona Lisa that she is the symbol of modern human nature, "of what in the ways of a thousand years
men had come to desire":

> Hers is the head upon which all "the ends of the world
> are come," and the eyelids are a little weary. It is a
> beauty wrought out from within upon the flesh, the de-
> posit, little cell by cell, of strange thoughts and fantastic
> reveries and exquisite passions. Set it for a moment beside
> one of those white Greek goddesses or beautiful women
> of antiquity, and how would they be troubled by this
> beauty, into which the soul with all its maladies has
> passed! . . .
> The fancy of a perpetual life, sweeping together ten
> thousand experiences, is an old one; and modern thought
> has conceived the idea of humanity as wrought upon by,
> and summing up in itself, all modes of thought and life.
> Certainly Lady Lisa might stand as the embodiment of
> the old fancy, the symbol of the modern idea. [*Renais-
> sance*, pp. 124–26]

If the Mona Lisa is Pater's symbol of the modern idea,
Sybil is Wilde's symbol of the old idea, gathering together ten
thousand experiences and embodying in herself the world's

purity. Dorian says of her: "I have seen her in every age and in every constume. Ordinary women never appeal to one's imagination. They are limited to their century" (*Gray*, p. 81). And again: "She is all the great heroines of the world in one. She is more than an individual" (*Gray*, p. 87). Pater had written of Greek art that it is too serene and undisturbed to satisfy us, for in ancient Greece the human race was still in its infancy, unaware of the seriousness and terror of evil and still uninfected by any spiritual sickness. Modern art, he held, must deal with the grotesque—with life, conflict, evil—for the evolution of the human spirit has made us terribly aware of the dark, evil caverns in human nature, and it is from this new situation that art must now try to wrest joy. The white Greek goddesses and beautiful women of antiquity no longer satisfy us.

Sybil, serene and untouched by any knowledge of evil, represents the Hellenic ideal. She has a "Greek head," and her name connects her with Greek mythology. When she appears in a play, it is invariably in the role of the spotless heroine— Juliet or Imogen or Rosalind—and Basil and Dorian see her purpose as that of spiritualizing the age. She is the visible symbol of an art and a state of the soul whose beauty is one of purity peculiar to the infancy of the race or of an age. Sybil exists in naturalistic surroundings—she acts in "an absurd little theatre, with great flaring gas-jets and gaudy play-bills," presided over by a "hideous Jew" who smokes "a vile cigar" (*Gray*, p. 77)—but her artistic imagination transforms her corrupt environment and renders it pure and spotless. Her imagination also transforms Dorian, for she sees him as entirely pure and untouched by evil at a time when he is already under Wotton's influence. For Sybil, Dorian is a fairy-tale prince out of the pages of literature:

> "She said quite simply to me, 'You look like a prince. I must call you Prince Charming.'"
> "Upon my word, Dorian, Miss Sybil knows how to pay compliments."

"You don't understand her, Harry. She regarded me
merely as a person in a play. She knows nothing of life."
[*Gray*, p. 85]

Sybil, however, is a child who cannot come of age and survive. She exists in a protective world of art from which she
cannot emerge without dying. Her projected marriage to
Dorian coaxes her out of this world and causes her to come
into contact with the demon universe. Pater, in the Conclusion to *The Renaissance*, maintained that success in life is to
achieve a state of constant ecstasy, to burn always with a hard,
gemlike flame, and ended his chapter thus:

> Great passions may give us this quickened sense of life,
> ecstasy and sorrow of love, the various forms of enthusias-
> tic activity, disinterested or otherwise, which come natu-
> rally to many of us. Only be sure it is passion—that it
> does yield you this fruit of a quickened, multiplied con-
> sciousness. Of this wisdom, the poetic passion, the desire
> of beauty, the love of art for art's sake, has most; for art
> comes to you professing frankly to give nothing but the
> highest quality to your moments as they pass, and simply
> for those moments' sake. [*Renaissance*, pp. 238–39]

It is art, then, that can give the highest quality to our moments, that can fire us with a constant flamelike ecstasy. Paradoxically, Sybil—in order to achieve this flamelike ecstasy—
rejects art for life, for a great passion. After she gives her terrible performance in front of Basil and Wotton, Dorian rushes
backstage to find that "the girl was standing there alone, with
a look of triumph on her face. Her eyes were lit with an
exquisite fire. There was a radiance about her. Her parted
lips were smiling over some secret of their own" (*Gray*, p. 135).
She says to him: "You have made me understand what love
really is. My love! my love! Prince Charming! Prince of life!
I have grown sick of shadows. You are more to me than all art
can ever be" (*Gray*, p. 137). Prince Charming is no longer a
character out of a play but is now the prince of life.

When Sybil's world of art is shattered, her imagination ceases to recreate the outside world and render it pure and spotless. As a consequence, she becomes aware of the sordid side of life:

> "To-night, for the first time in my life, I saw through the hollowness, the sham, the silliness of the empty pageant in which I had always played. To-night, for the first time, I became conscious that the Romeo was hideous, and old, and painted, that the moonlight in the orchard was false, that the scenery was vulgar, and that the words I had to speak were unreal, were not my words, were not what I wanted to say." [*Gray*, p. 137]

Sybil, however, is too fragile to confront the demonic and survive. The death blow falls when she becomes aware of the evil in Dorian. Dorian had loved her as an erotic symbol of purity, but when she rejects art for life, she loses her ability to isolate herself from "the stain of an age . . . at once sordid and sensual." Like the protagonists of the fairy tales, she moves from innocence into experience, but as soon as she enters the demonic world of the naturalists, she begins to have naturalistic experiences. Dorian callously walks out on her, and she dies by swallowing "some dreadful thing they use at theatres," with white lead or prussic acid in it. Her lonely suicide in a tawdry actress's dressing room is straight Zola. This is how people die in naturalist literature—not on the high seas or in Horatio's arms, but alone, in poverty and despair. Wotton reflects on her death, "The moment she touched actual life she marred it, and it marred her, and so she passed away" (*Gray*, p. 165).

Sybil's death has dimensions that far transcend her death as the result of a psychological state. "Without your art you are nothing" (*Gray*, p. 139), Dorian informs her, and indeed her death symbolizes the death of an entire movement in art. Sybil is inseparable from art. Dorian says:

> "On the first night I was at the theatre, the horrid old Jew came round to the box after the performance was

over, and offered to take me behind the scenes and introduce me to her. I was furious with him, and told him that
Juliet had been dead for hundreds of years, and that her
body was lying in a marble tomb in Verona. I think, from
his blank look of amazement, that he was under the impression that I had taken too much champagne, or something." [*Gray*, p. 83]

Pater saw the Mona Lisa as the supreme example of modern art, for modern art must encompass all of human nature,
in all its evil and terror, and present it in a way that makes it
beautiful. He saw the portrait of *La Gioconda* as combining
in its chill beauty the pure and evil strains in human nature—
as summing up human nature from a modern perspective.
Humanity, for Pater, has developed beyond its initial state of
innocence and can no longer be satisfied with an art that cannot deal with evil. Wilde, in *Dorian Gray*, modifies Pater's
idea and applies it to the Victorian world as a separate entity,
as though the human race had been born anew at the beginning of the Victorian period. Iain Fletcher has observed that
"Pater's method, in *The Renaissance*," is to explore "not so
much a period as a movement of history through selected individuals." [6] Wilde's method is the same, but he focuses instead on the movement of a single period, presenting the Victorians as having begun in placid innocence but developed beyond it.

Sybil is the symbol of the innocence of the Victorians, both
in life and in art. She represents a movement in art that knows
nothing of evil and dwells in a beautiful, private world. In
this respect, she suggests Tennyson more than anyone else.
The early Tennyson wrote poetry that was serenely unaware
of evil and that advocated an isolated existence in a dazzling,
beautiful world of art. It is precisely such a world that the
poet seeks and finds in "Recollections of the Arabian Nights."
The ivory tower of serene artistic delight is very much the
message of Tennyson's early poetry. "The Palace of Art" and

6. Iain Fletcher, *Walter Pater* (London: Longmans, Green and Co.,
1959), p. 16.

"The Lady of Shalott," however, reflect his growing dissatisfac-
tion with this private world. And in *In Memoriam*, the
beautiful art world crumbles and Tennyson confronts the
demonic, mid-Victorian scientific universe.

Like Sybil, moreover, Tennyson tumbles from his ivory
tower into the demon universe because of a great love. Unlike
Sybil, though, he paradoxically survives to retreat into the
world of Arthurian romance and to write about a virtuous
king who is finally destroyed by evil forces outside himself.
Interestingly, "The Last Tournament," one of the grimmest
and darkest of the Idylls, was published in 1872, and Tennyson at the time meant it as the continuation and conclusion of
The Idylls of the King ("The Passing of Arthur" had appeared earlier, in 1869). In 1885, he published another Idyll,
"Balin and Balan," but that was to appear toward the middle
of the sequence, not—like "The Passing of Arthur" and "The
Last Tournament"—at the end. *The Idylls of the King* may
be said to be Tennyson's last great work. Much of his time
after 1872 was devoted to an unsuccessful attempt to storm the
English stage with a series of historical tragedies, until in 1884
he gave up in despair! [7]

It is probably the art movement of Tennyson that Sybil is
meant to represent. He looked to past ages and foreign lands
in his poetry, and Sybil always appears in plays belonging to
past centuries and set in foreign lands. Her relationship with
Dorian, moreover, clearly suggests the Lady of Shalott, and
she indeed echoes her when she rejects art and says to her
lover, "I have grown sick of shadows." The art of an age can
isolate itself from evil only during the infancy of that age. As
the age matures, such art movements must collapse as evil
presses in on them. Consequently Sybil, the symbol of an innocent movement in Victorian art, dies. The Satanic Wotton

7. In 1884, Tennyson disclaimed any hope of "meeting the exigencies
of our modern theatre." His attempt to storm the stage coincides with
Sybil's rejection of it. Apart from Wilde's stylistic carelessness in *Dorian
Gray* and his inadequate treatment of the passage of time, the book's
chief fault is that it is far too heavily paradoxical.

reflects: "There is something to me quite beautiful about her death. I am glad I am living in a century when such wonders happen" (*Gray*, p. 164).

Sybil's mother and brother, like Sybil, represent a trend in art that belongs to the innocence of the Victorians, and they too are inseparable from the movement they symbolize. Wilde tells us of Jim Vane: "He was thick-set of figure, and his hands and feet were large, and somewhat clumsy in movement. He was not so finely bred as his sister. One would hardly have guessed the close relationship that existed between them" (*Gray*, p. 98). And yet a very close relationship does exist. Whereas Sybil represented the innocence of the Victorians at a very high artistic level, Jim represents the same thing at a much lower level. James Vane and his mother are straight out of Victorian melodrama, and Victorian melodrama, in its infantile treatment of evil, its lack of intellectual content, its presentation of heroes who always triumph and black villains who are always defeated, is a drama of childlike innocence. Jim Vane is not an individual but a type. To Sybil's artistic imagination, he is all the heroes of Victorian melodrama rolled into one. His future is envisioned by his sister:

> He was to leave the vessel at Melbourne, bid a polite good-bye to the captain, and go off at once to the gold-fields. Before a week was over he was to come across a large nugget of pure gold, the largest nugget that had ever been discovered, and bring it down to the coast in a waggon guarded by six mounted policemen. The bushrangers were to attack them three times, and be defeated with immense slaughter. Or, no. He was not to go to the gold-fields at all. They were horrid places, where men got intoxicated, and shot each other in bar-rooms, and used bad language. He was to be a nice sheep-farmer, and one evening, as he was riding home, he was to see the beautiful heiress being carried off by a robber on a black horse, and give chase, and rescue her. Of course she would fall in love with him, and he with her, and they would get

married, and come home, and live in an immense house
in London. Yes, there were delightful things in store for
him. [*Gray*, pp. 104–05]

The specific events in Jim's future are uncertain, but what
is certain is that there are delightful, melodramatic things in
store for him. And indeed, if he were acting in a melodrama
there would be no question about that. Jim's tragedy, however, is similar to his sister's: he rejects art for life. Instead
of joining the group, as his mother had wished, he decides to
become a real-life sailor and says to his mother: "I should like
to make some money to take you and Sybil off the stage. I hate
it" (*Gray*, p. 99). By rejecting the stage, however, he becomes
part of the terrible world of the naturalists. He continues to
behave melodramatically in this world, making wild threats
against Sybil's aristocratic lover, and Sybil says to him: "Oh,
don't be so serious, Jim. You are like one of the heroes of
those silly melodramas mother used to be so fond of acting
in" (*Gray*, p. 110). When we meet Jim again, nearly eighteen
years later, he is associated with loathsome dens, dark alleys,
old hags, and the filth of port life. This is the world of the
naturalists, but he continues to behave melodramatically in it.
He is mistakenly shot and killed while hiding behind a bush
—an unthinkable end for a stout-hearted British sailor in a
proper melodrama, but a very usual end for a character in
naturalist literature.

Sybil's mother is a secondary character, but she is a counterpoint to her son in that she is a melodramatic figure who
clings on to the stage. She yearns for the days when melodrama
was popular, and she compensates by trying to mold her life
into a melodrama. This is how she reacts to Sybil:

> "Ah! mother, mother, let me be happy!"
> Mrs. Vane glanced at her, and with one of those false
> theatrical gestures that so often becomes a mode of second
> nature to a stage-player, clasped her in her arms. [*Gray*,
> p. 98]

And again:

> "Kiss me, mother," said the girl. Her flower-like lips
> touched the withered cheek, and warmed its frost.
> "My child! my child!" cried Mrs. Vane, looking up to
> the ceiling in search of an imaginary gallery. [*Gray*,
> p. 103]

Mrs. Vane absolutely must exist in a melodramatic atmosphere. She has outlived her time, however, and she suggests more than anything else a defeated character in a naturalistic novel. The "silly melodramas" she "used to be so fond of acting in" were probably of the *Black-Eyed Susan* and *Luke the Labourer* variety. As early as the 1860s, these crude melodramas were already on the decline. "By the 1860's melodramas were simply better written than they had been earlier. Characters remained types, but touches of subtlety and complexity appeared in characterization. Slapstick was replaced by witty repartee. Restrained sentiment now and then replaced tear-jerking sentimentality." [8] The sordid world of the naturalists, moreover, infiltrated the melodrama in the 1860s and began to make appearances in the plays of Boucicault—in his famous melodrama, *After Dark*, for instance. By the 1890s, the old-fashioned branch of the melodrama had died out. The new and more vigorous branch had evolved into the new drama.[9] Mrs. Vane dies after her daughter but before her son. Indeed, Wilde presents her as in a sense already dead, for she is old and withered and decayed. The Victorians having emerged from their state of innocence, melodrama is inevitably in a state of decay, moving toward certain death.

Sybil's rejection of art and her subsequent suicide constitute a further deliverance of Dorian into the hands of the devil. Dorian says to Wotton at one point, concerning Sybil:

8. Introduction to *British Plays of the Nineteenth Century*, ed. J. O. Bailey (New York: Odyssey Press, 1966), p. 34.
9. Ibid.

"And her voice—I never heard such a voice. It was very low at first, with deep mellow notes, that seemed to fall singly upon one's ear. Then it became a little louder, and sounded like a flute or a distant hautbois. In the garden-scene it had all the tremulous ecstasy that one hears just before dawn when nightingales are singing. There were moments, later on, when it had the wild passion of violins. You know how a voice can stir one. Your voice and the voice of Sybil Vane are two things I shall never forget. When I close my eyes, I hear them, and each of them says something different. I don't know which to follow." [*Gray,* pp. 80–81]

The passage recalls an earlier one, already quoted, giving Dorian's reaction to Wotton's voice. Dorian's nature is gray: good and evil are locked in mortal combat within him. Wotton is the voice of evil, while Sybil, reinforced by Basil, is the voice of goodness. When Sybil dies, Basil becomes exclusively the voice of goodness for Dorian, but the voice comes primarily from within Dorian, and the murder of Basil, instead of silencing it, only intensifies it. It is Dorian's destiny, however, to yield to the evil voice within himself. He has, after all, sold his soul to the devil:

"I wish now I had not told you about Sybil Vane."

"You could not have helped telling me, Dorian. All through your life you will tell me everything you do."

"Yes, Harry, I believe that is true. I cannot help telling you things. You have a curious influence over me." [*Gray,* p. 82]

At one point, Lord Henry Wotton says to Dorian: "A new Hedonism—that is what our century wants. You might be its visible symbol" (*Gray,* p. 35). It is Dorian's destiny to be the perfect embodiment of this new hedonism—of decadence.

Before Sybil's death, Dorian searches for pure sensations. After her death, the sensations he seeks become less and less pure. He falls heavily under the spell of a mysterious yellow

book—usually identified as Huysmans's *À Rebours*—and this
is a crucial stage in his development as a decadent, although it
is only chapter 11 and the final pages of chapter 10 that record
the yellow book's evil influence. Since the yellow book forms
such an important stage in Dorian's development, it is necessary to understand what Wilde meant it to suggest. Wilde
wrote, in chapter 11, that one has "ancestors in literature, as
well as in one's own race, nearer perhaps in type and tempera-
ment, many of them, and certainly with an influence of which
one was more absolutely conscious" (*Gray*, p. 232).

The two major influences on the English decadent movement were Pater's *The Renaissance* (1873) and Joris-Karl
Huysmans's *À Rebours* (1884). The yellow book is a nonexis-
tent combination of these two works, one English and the other
French; Dorian, it will be recalled, was born of an English
father and a French mother. Although chapter 11 mostly reflects *À Rebours,* strong echoes of *The Renaissance* also occur,
mostly toward the beginning. Dorian remains under the spell
of the yellow book for eighteen years, moreover, and if we accept that he died in 1890—the year in which most of *The
Picture of Dorian Gray* was written and the earlier version
published—then it becomes impossible to see the yellow book
as being simply *À Rebours* and very easy to recognize it as
also being partly *The Renaisssance.*

Through the yellow book and because of it, the post-Sybil
Dorian experiences the history of the entire human race, precisely as Huysmans's hero did, and learns everything that
Pater asserted modern man already knows: "It seemed to him
that in exquisite raiment, and to the delicate sound of flutes,
the sins of the world were passing in dumb show before him.
Things that he had dimly dreamed of were suddenly made
real to him. Things of which he had never dreamed were gradually revealed" (*Gray*, p. 201). Finally, Dorian comes to feel
that he has absorbed everything the human race has ever
known, especially its evil passions and sensations: "There were
times when it seemed to Dorian Gray that the whole of history

was merely the record of his own life, not as he had lived it
in act and circumstance, but as his imagination had created it
for him, as it had been in his brain and in his passions. He
felt that he had known them all, those strange terrible figures
that had passed across the stage of the world and made sin so
marvellous and evil so full of subtlety. It seemed to him that
in some mysterious way their lives had been his own" (*Gray*,
pp. 232–33).

Dorian, however, will go beyond anything the race—in-
cluding Des Esseintes and the modern Paterian man—has yet
known, and will become the visible symbol of Wotton's new
hedonism. The yellow book teaches him an important lesson.
Wilde ends chapter 11 thus: "Dorian Gray had been poisoned
by a book. There were moments when he looked on evil simply as a mode through which he could realise his conception
of the beautiful" (*Gray*, p. 236). The book teaches Dorian to
seek beauty in evil, and as he comes to depend more and more
on evil and evil sensations in his search for beauty, he becomes a full-blown decadent. Along with the detailed record
in chapter 11 of Dorian's interest in jewels and perfumes,
lengthy and mysterious absences are mentioned, after which
he creeps back home, goes to the locked room and gazes with
joy at his grinning, sin-scarred portrait, the mirror of his soul,
gleefully comparing it with the beautiful mask that is his
body: "He grew more and more enamoured of his own beauty,
more and more interested in the corruption of his own soul.
He would examine with minute care, and sometimes with a
monstrous and terrible delight, the hideous lines that seared
the wrinkling forehead or crawled around the heavy sensual
mouth, wondering sometimes which were the more horrible,
the signs of sin or the signs of age" (*Gray*, p. 206; italics mine).
The portrait is in the process of becoming a decadent work of
art. The hideous, evil portrait, and Dorian's gleeful reaction
to it, typifies a very important aspect of that art—the delighted recognition and celebration of the evil within the
soul. We later learn—just before Basil's murder—that the
portrait has "grinning lips." Decadent art, like aesthetic art,

deals to a large extent with the world within, but while moral aesthetic art—Rossetti's is the major example—presents the soul as being essentially pure, decadent art sees it as being evil and derives pleasure from this evil. The decadent poetry of Arthur Symons, for instance, is largely a sensually rendered exploration—often a celebration —of the poet's "spiritual and moral perversity." [10] Enid Starkie, in *From Gautier to Eliot,* has noted the influence of the French symbolist movement on Symons's decadent poetry. [11] In "The Decadent Movement in Literature" (1893), Symons did not much differentiate between the terms *decadent* and *symbolist,* and he described decadence as a "beautiful and interesting disease." [12] More recently, James Nelson, in *The Early Nineties: A View From the Bodley Head,* has examined the poems of *Silhouettes* (1892) and found them in the French impressionist and symbolist vein, the chief influence being Verlaine. Nelson tells us that "Symons was fascinated by the whirling sights, the silhouettes dark against the light of the gas jets, the smoke, the talk, and the music of the café-dance hall and found in such haunts men like puppets abandoning themselves to a kind of madness and oblivion born of disillusionment and despair. But perhaps of even more interest to him was the kind of beauty found there, a tainted beauty all the more fascinating and significant for its signs of evil and artifice." [13] In "Javanese Dancers," which Nelson rightly calls "a symbolist poem," he finds "Symons' most potent evocation of an evil beauty comparable to something perhaps only Beardsley could create." [14] The poem's central

10. Arthur Symons, "The Decadent Movement in Literature," *Harper's New Monthly Magazine* 87 (November, 1893): 858–67. In the essay Symons defined decadence as "an intense self-consciousness, a restless curiosity in research, an over-subtilising refinement upon refinement, a spiritual and moral perversity."

11. Enid Starkie, *From Gautier to Eliot,* pp. 107–20.

12. Symons, "The Decadent Movement in Literature."

13. James G. Nelson, *The Early Nineties: A View From the Bodley Head* (Cambridge, Mass.: Harvard University Press, 1971), p. 191.

14. Ibid., p. 194.

dancer, who radiates a strange, bewitchingly demonic beauty, appears on the stage

> Smiling between her painted lids a smile
> Motionless, unintelligible, she twines
> Her fingers into mazy lines,
> Twining her scarves across them all the while.[15]

As Nelson observes, this central dancer is "essentially what Frank Kermode has described as the Romantic Image." [16] Her sensuous, undulating form is a symbol of perfect harmony, fusing together the opposites of body and soul, of the outer world Symons is contemplating and the world within himself. Her body, which Symons worships, is also that fascinating disease, his own corrupt soul.

If the poems of *Silhouettes* are largely dominated by a gray mood of pessimism, those of *London Nights* (1895) are unified by a heated, hungry sensuality. These poems must not be read simply as a celebration of lust, however. The voluptuous harlots and abandoned women who fill the pages of *London Nights* are heavily sensuous, erotic symbols in the outer world of Symons's tainted, evil soul. In the opening poem of the volume, "Prologue," Symons indicates to us how the poems of *London Nights* should be approached. The tone of "Prologue" is one of dismay rather than delight, but the symbols are clearly identified as such:

> My life is like a music-hall,
> Where, in the impotence of rage,
> Chained by enchantment to my stall,
> I see myself upon the stage
> Dance to amuse a music-hall.

15. Arthur Symons, *Silhouettes*, p. 41. "Javanese Dancers" was later revised by Symons.

16. Nelson, *The Early Nineties*, p. 194. See also Frank Kermode, *Romantic Image* (London: Routledge and Kegan Paul, 1957), especially chapter 3, "The Image."

'Tis I that smoke this cigarette,
Lounge here, and laugh for vacancy,
And watch the dancers turn; and yet
It is my very self I see
Across the cloudy cigarette.

My very self that turns and trips,
Painted, pathetically gay,
An empty song upon the lips
In make-believe of holiday:
I, I, this thing that turns and trips!

The light flares in the music-hall,
The light, the sound, that weary us;
Hour follows hour, I count them all,
Lagging, and loud, and riotous:
My life is like a music-hall.[17]

In the brief but important preface to the second edition of
London Nights, Symons suggests that "the whole visible world
. . . is but a symbol, made visible in order that we may ap-
prehend ourselves, and not be blown hither and thither like
a flame in the night." [18] Symons recognized the painted dancers he sought in music halls and the harlots he embraced as being symbols in the visible world of the soul within himself,
and the poems of *London Nights*—for all their heated sensuality—attempt to go beneath the surface of things to explore
and celebrate the perverse, evil world within. In "Stella
Maris," [19] for instance (which first appeared separately in *The
Yellow Book* in 1894), Symons celebrates a night of delirious
lust as "that ineffable delight/ When souls turn bodies, and
unite/ In the intolerable, the whole/ Rapture of the embodied soul." In "Liber Amoris," [20] he informs us that once,

17. Arthur Symons, *London Nights,* p. 3.
18. Symons, *London Nights,* 2d rev. ed. (London: Leonard Smithers,
1897), p. xiv.
19. Symons, *London Nights,* 1st ed., pp. 40–41.
20. Ibid., pp. 100–03.

long ago, "I loved good women," but adds ironically that,
"for a body and soul like mine,/ I found the angels' food too
fine."
The soul seeks that in the visible world which most ap-
proximates its own nature, and instead of worshiping blessed
damozels like Rossetti, Symons yields passionately to lust and
vice, adoring, rather, the seductive Bianca, whose "illusive
change,/ The strangeness of your smile, the faint/ Corruption
of your gaze," is reminiscent of the Mona Lisa as described in
Pater's *Renaissance*. He ends his poem with the daring line,
"So Bianca satisfies my soul." Like Dorian, Symons seems to
have "had mad hungers that grew more ravenous as he fed
them" (*Gray*, p. 207), but also like Dorian, he was at this point
very deeply "interested in the corruption of his own soul."
Similarly, John Gray, in the poems that make up his volume
of decadent verse, *Silverpoints* (1893), has for one of his main
themes the identification and celebration of the evil within
the human soul. Here is one of the best of his poems, titled
simply "Poem":

> Geranium, houseleek, laid in oblong beds
> On the trim grass. The daisies' leprous stain
> Is fresh. Each night the daisies burst again,
> Though every day the gardener crops their heads.
>
> A wistful child, in foul unwholesome shreds,
> Recalls some legend of a daisy chain
> That makes a pretty necklace. She would fain
> Make one, and wear it, if she had some threads.
>
> Sun, leprous flowers, foul child. The asphalt burns.
> The garrulous sparrows perch on metal Burns.
> Sing! Sing! they say, and flutter with their wings.
> He does not sing, he only wonders why
> He is sitting there. The sparrows sing. And I
> Yield to the strait allure of simple things.[21]

21. John Gray, *Silverpoints*, p. xx.

In the first stanza, nature is represented as evil. The gardener attempts to suppress and control the evil daisies, but every night they burst again and their leprous stain remains fresh. In the second stanza, a child recalls some vague, romantic legend about daisies—Wordsworth's "To the Daisy" poems come to mind here [22]—but the child, ironically, is foul and yearns to make "a pretty necklace" of the leprous flowers, and wear it around her neck. In the third stanza, the life-giving sun, leprous flowers, and foul child unite to form an unholy trinity. The sun is scorching and it makes the asphalt—a symbol of civilization—burn with its oppressive heat. The metal statue of Burns is totally out of place in this un-Romantic setting, but the garrulous sparrows, symbols of uncontrolled nature, are quite at home, and they sing as they perch on the silent statue of the Romantic poet.

This garden setting is entirely in accord with the evil nature of John Gray, and he ends his poem by yielding happily "to the strait allure of simple things." In "Poem," Gray celebrates evil, locates it both within himself and in the outside world, and embraces it. Almost a century before, Wordsworth had "heard a thousand blended notes,/ While in a grove I sate reclined," and had said that "To her fair works did Nature link/ The human soul that through me ran." [23] Gray's human

22. Wordsworth had ended his best "To the Daisy" poem with the following stanza:

> Child of the Year! that round dost run
> Thy pleasant course,—when day's begun
> As ready to salute the sun
>   As lark or leveret,
> Thy long-lost praise thou shalt regain
> Than in old time:—thou not in vain
>   Art Nature's favourite.

Chaucer and the early poets had paid many honors to the daisy. Words-worth revives this tradition and hopes that future men will also love and praise the daisy. If Gray's verses are read in the light of Wordsworth's hope, then the deeply ironic nature of "Poem" gains a new dimension.

23. Wordsworth, "Lines Written in Early Spring."

soul links with a nature that is the antithesis of Wordsworth's
—a nature thrilling with evil beauty.

Dorian's grinning, evil portrait, then, and his delighted reaction to it, is typical of one very important aspect of decadent
art—the gleeful recognition and celebration of a depravity
whose wellsprings are within the soul.

The Pre-Raphaelite movement in England, dominated by
the figure of Dante Gabriel Rossetti, began toward the middle
of the nineteenth century and was on the wane by 1890. In
The Picture of Dorian Gray, Basil Hallward is the representative of this movement. In his very photographic approach to
painting, Basil suggests Holman Hunt, and perhaps also John
Everett Millais, both members of the original Pre-Raphaelite
Brotherhood. Jerome Buckley has observed of Hunt that "to
perceive intensely and to paint with absolute 'truth to nature'
were the first principles of his Pre-Raphaelite creed." In his
paintings, Hunt strove for absolute authenticity in every last
detail. For instance, "The Scapegoat" was "modelled by a real
goat tethered in woebegone thirst by the actual shore of the
Dead Sea." The background of "The Triumph of the Inno-
cents," moreover, was "drawn with photographic fidelity on
the very road from Jerusalem to Bethlehem." [24]

Basil, however, largely suggests Rossetti. Buckley has written
of Rossetti: "Both as painter and as poet, Rossetti, though at-
tentive always to detail, was more literary than literal, interested first of all in the psychology of moods, the analysis of
states of soul, and eager to depict the life of an imagination
nourished on books and private reverie." Far more anxiously
than his disciples, however, "Rossetti sought to make the
sharp sense impression the avenue to mystical revelation." [25]
In his paintings and writings, Rossetti presented women
chiefly as sensuous manifestations of total spiritual purity—a
purity he deeply yearned for and found personified in Elizabeth Siddal and Jane Morris. In Rossetti's early short story,

24. Jerome H. Buckley, introduction to *The Pre-Raphaelites,* ed.
Jerome H. Buckley (New York: Modern Library, 1968), p. xvii.
25. Ibid., pp. xx–xxi.

"Hand and Soul," the beautiful, ethereal lady who appears in Chiaro's room and bids him serve God by painting her, identifies herself as his soul. There was a demonic streak in Rossetti's soul, however, and this is vividly expressed, for instance, in his portrait of Lilith. Basil, in painting and worshiping Dorian as the sensuous manifestation of his largely pure but tainted soul—the painting contains a tinge of evil—clearly suggests Rossetti, although he worships a beautiful boy instead of a beautiful lady.

In *The Renaissance,* however, Pater had presented the Victorian world with a new kind of artist, one who owed much to the Pre-Raphaelites but who could best be characterized as a decadent. Instead of painting and worshiping blessed, ethereal ladies, Pater's Leonardo—the type of the modern artist—had been fascinated, rather, by the head of the Medusa. Pater informs us of Leonardo's depiction of this terrible head: "The subject has been treated in various ways; Leonardo alone cuts to its centre; he alone realises it as the head of a corpse, exercising its powers through all the circumstances of death. What may be called the fascination of corruption penetrates in every touch its exquisitely finished beauty. About the dainty lines of the cheek the bat flits unheeded. The delicate snakes seem literally strangling each other in terrified struggle to escape from the Medusa brain" (*Renaissance,* p. 106). Leonardo plunged into the depths of "human personality and became above all a painter of portraits." In the bewitchingly evil, enigmatic, smiling face of the Mona Lisa, he found and captured on canvas the perfect expression of human personality as Pater felt the modern world has come to know it.

Insofar as one can generalize about the Pre-Raphaelite movement, it is possible to maintain that its fortunes after 1873 were on the decline. Rossetti, the chief Pre-Raphaelite, had two periods of intense creativity. The first occurred in the 1850s, the second around 1868. Most of the poems that comprise his masterpiece, *The House of Life,* were written between 1868 and 1870. However, Robert Buchanan's attack on him in "The Fleshly School of Poetry," which first appeared in the *Contemporary Review* in October, 1871, cut deep. Already "nervously debilitated, he now felt relentlessly persecuted by a whole Philistine world he had never cared to understand. Henceforth he was increasingly subject to delusive fears and more or less constant insomnia." [26] He continued to write and paint until his death in 1882, and his reputation continued to spread as he attracted more and more disciples, but Rossetti himself was in a state of decline and no one of equal stature appeared to carry on the torch.

John Ruskin is another major figure one associates with the Pre-Raphaelites, though he was definitely separate from them. Ruskin was the chief promoter and defender of the early Pre-Raphaelites—Rossetti especially—and the author of the voluminous work, *Modern Painters* (1843–60), upon which the original Pre-Raphaelites looked with admiration. He fervently believed, moreover, that art and morality are inseparable. Richard Ellmann has observed of Basil: "The painter Hallward has little of Ruskin at the beginning [of *Dorian Gray*], but gradually he moves closer to that pillar of esthetic taste and moral judgment upon which Wilde leaned, and after Hallward is safely murdered, Dorian with sudden fondness recollects a trip they had made to Venice together, when his friend was captured by Tintoretto's art. Ruskin was of course the English discoverer and champion of Tintoretto, so that the allusion is specific." [27]

In 1882, however, the youthful Oscar Wilde himself, speaking in the name of the new, amoral aesthetes of the 1880s, wrote that "we of the younger school have made a departure from the teachings of Mr. Ruskin,—a departure definite and different and decisive. . . . In his art criticism, his estimate of the joyous element of art, his whole method of approaching art, we are no longer with him; for the keystone to his aesthetic system is ethical always. He would judge of a picture by the amount of noble moral ideas it expresses." In the same essay—titled "L'Envoi"—Wilde declared that "the ultimate

26. Buckley, ed., *The Pre-Raphaelites*, p. 4.
27. Richard Ellmann, "Overtures to *Salome*," p. 88.

expression of our artistic movement in painting has been, not in the spiritual visions of the Pre-Raphaelites, for all their marvel of Greek legend and their mystery of Italian song, but in the work of such men as Whistler and Albert Moore, who have raised design and colour to the ideal level of poetry and music" (*Miscellanies*, pp. 30–32).

Wilde, in the essay, connects Ruskin with the Pre-Raphaelites and sees both as linking art with morality. Moreover, in 1878 Ruskin suffered the first of seven attacks of madness that culminated in 1889 with the most damaging one. Ruskin's recurring fits of insanity interfered seriously with his work, and after 1889 he wrote practically nothing and spent the rest of his life in mute retirement. As this was occurring, the decadent movement, sparked by *The Renaissance* and inspired from across the channel by writers such as Baudelaire, Verlaine, Mallarmé, and Huysmans, was gaining momentum. By 1890, it was clearly emerging as an important movement in literature, and the stage was set for the appearance of an Aubrey Beardsley in painting.

The steady deterioration of Basil Hallward as an artist between 1873 and the time of his death on a dark, foggy November night in 1889, is meant to symbolize the decline of Rossetti, Pre-Raphaelitism in general, and Ruskin's "Moral Aesthetic." [28] At the beginning of *Dorian Gray*, Basil had made a

28. Jerome Hamilton Buckley, *The Victorian Temper* (Cambridge, Mass.: Harvard University Press, 1951). See chapter 8, "The Moral Aesthetic," which is an excellent introduction to Ruskin. Buckley is not always excellent in *The Victorian Temper*, however. In chapter 11, "The 'Aesthetic' Eighties," he oversimplifies the decade considerably. At one point in "The 'Aesthetic' Eighties," though, he makes a first-rate observation about the latter-day aesthetes who separated art from morality: "If *Patience* exposed to Philistine laughter their obvious mannerisms, it left untouched the first principles of art for art's sake. In *The North Wall* (1885), an early prose-satire by John Davidson, the Aesthetes might perhaps have found a somewhat subtler attack on their basic faith. Eager to live the novel he is unable to write, Davidson's hero feels forced 'to execute atrocities which, committed selfishly, would brand the criminal as an unnatural monster, but which, performed for art's sake, will rebound everlastingly to the credit of the artist.' But even if they had come by

request of Wotton: "Don't take away from me the one person who gives to my art whatever charm it possesses: my life as an artist depends on him" (*Gray*, p. 22). Wotton did not heed the request, and Basil's art consistently deteriorated as Dorian— symbol incarnate of the painter's soul—drifted away from him. It is not until Dorian reveals his true soul to Basil in the sinister thirteenth chapter of the novel, however, that the painter is completely destroyed as an artist:

> Hallward turned again to the portrait, and gazed at it. "My God, if it is true," he exclaimed, "and this is what you have done with your life, why, you must be worse even than those who talk against you fancy you to be!" He held the light up again to the canvas, and examined it. The surface seemed to be quite undisturbed, and as he had left it. It was from within, apparently, that the foulness and horror had come. Through some strange quickening of inner life the leprosies of sin were slowly eating the thing away. The rotting of a corpse in a watery grave was not so fearful.
>
> His hand shook, and the candle fell from its socket on the floor, and lay there sputtering. He placed his foot on it and put it out. Then he flung himself into the rickety chair that was standing by the table and buried his face in his hands. [*Gray*, pp. 253–54]

Basil represents an art movement that recognizes the evil within the self and deals seriously with it, but can accept it only in small doses. When the soul reveals itself as overwhelmingly evil, Ruskin, or the Pre-Raphaelite artist, can only shrink away in horror and yield to the decadent, who can accept this vision and wring satisfaction from it. Basil's murder

odd chance upon this burlesque, few among the intense young men would as yet have grasped the truth of its intimation that a consistently 'amoral' art must lead at last to the inverted moralities of Decadence." Wilde, in "The Young King," showed an intense awareness of the fact that an amoral art can lead in the end to decadence, and insisted that the highest art is inseparable from utter spiritual purity—a position he rejected in *Dorian Gray*.

is not only the murder of one human being by another but also the murder of Pre-Raphaelite art and the Ruskinian "Moral Aesthetic" by decadent art. The horror on the canvas is specifically presented as an accomplice in the murder:

> Dorian Gray glanced at the picture, and suddenly an uncontrollable feeling of hatred for Basil Hallward came over him, as though it had been suggested to him by the image on the canvas, whispered into his ear by those grinning lips. The mad passions of a hunted animal stirred within him, and he loathed the man who was seated at the table, more than in his whole life he had ever loathed anything. . . . He rushed at him, and dug the knife into the great vein that is behind the ear, crushing the man's head down on the table, and stabbing again and again. [*Gray*, pp. 255–56]

Dorian murders Basil because of an uncontrollable passion for sin, an insane desire to destroy the man who is praying and asking him to go down on his knees and pray too. The murder is an attempt on Dorian's part to stifle the voice of goodness forever. The picture's complicity in the murder, however, gives the act an added dimension: decadent art, having replaced Pre-Raphaelite art on the canvas and destroyed—even inverted—the Ruskinian link between art and morality, now completes the job by murdering the Pre-Raphaelite artist who, Ruskin-like, is praying to God. Quite probably, Wilde must have seen Ruskin's serious and very damaging attack of madness in the autumn of 1889 as effectively marking the end of an entire movement in art—certainly the end of the idea that art and morality are somehow wedded, an idea found not only in Ruskin but "in the spiritual visions of the Pre-Raphaelites" as well.[29]

The murder of Basil is the turning point for Dorian. The

29. Literary history is not that simple, however. In fact, Pre-Raphaelitism survived into the 1890s, and, Beardsley still had to submit to it and invert it in his "Incipit Vita Nuova" of 1892. The autumn of 1889, however, does very definitely mark the effective end of John Ruskin as a writer and thinker.

portrait records this evil act, and Dorian begins to lose his nerve. The sight of so much evil becomes intolerable even to him, and he finds himself unable to derive pleasure from his new sin:

> He felt that if he brooded on what he had gone through he would sicken or grow mad. There were sins whose fascination was more in the memory than in the doing of them, strange triumphs that gratified the pride more than the passions, and gave to the intellect a quickened sense of joy, greater than any joy they brought, or could ever bring, to the senses. But this was not one of them. It was a thing to be driven out of the mind, to be drugged with poppies, to be strangled lest it might strangle one itself. [*Gray*, p. 262]

"Poppies" fail to strangle Dorian's sense of horror, though, and his encounter with Jim Vane shatters his nerves. The voice of goodness wells up from within him, poisoning his existence. He decides to escape by retracing his steps, by becoming once again a pure, innocent being, and his first good action is to spare a country girl. Wotton, however, suggests to him that the action was simply an attempt to experience a new sensation, and the portrait corroborates this by becoming more hideous. Dorian examines his motives closely and decides that this was indeed the case. Dorian, in this respect, is a typical decadent. Having yielded to the evil in himself, he ultimately discovers, to his horror, that he can no longer derive pleasure from it and that the plunge into the demon universe has become an irreversible process. Trapped in this demonic underworld, he has only one road of escape left, and that is death.

It is a road that Alan Campbell before him had taken. Alan had been corrupted by Dorian, but withdrew from a life of sin and decided to give expression to his corrupt impulses only within the framework of science, cutting up corpses and experimenting on rotting bodies. Dorian, however, brings him to a terrible and unbearable confrontation with evil—a confrontation Alan could not have possibly avoided—and the result is Alan's suicide. This is the inevitable end of the decadent, and Alan's suicide presages Dorian's death. Dorian, unable to bear the sight of his hideous portrait any longer, and identifying it with his conscience, decides to destroy it. For Dorian, this is the ultimate evil act, the desire to rid himself of all moral sense. The attempt to escape through good actions having failed, he decides to escape by committing the most terrible of crimes. When he plunges the blade into his "monstrous soul-life," however, he kills himself—this is really his only way out.

Wotton remains alive, but his fate, paradoxically, is the worst in the novel and is foreshadowed when his wife deserts him. Wotton's wife is not an individual but a type. Wilde says of her: "She was usually in love with somebody, and, as her passion was never returned, she had kept all her illusions. She tried to look picturesque, but only succeeded in being untidy. Her name was Victoria, and she had a perfect mania for going to church" (*Gray*, pp. 71–72). She is the Victorian world personified, and Wotton's marriage to her is as necessary to his well-being as the dinner parties he attends. The paradoxist must have a fixed standard of values if he is to create paradoxes. Wotton as paradoxist continually stands Victorian values on their heads, but his marriage to Victoria is necessary if he is to continue to do this.

Unfortunately for Wotton, the continual process of inverting Victorian values ultimately destroys those values, and Victoria finally commits the very un-Victorian act of eloping. This, however, merely foreshadows Wotton's loss of his artistic masterpiece, Dorian, into whom he had poured all his soul. Wotton's paradoxes were only the means to an end—they were the evil brush he used to refashion Dorian in the light of his own soul. It should be stressed that Wotton has entirely renounced evil in his life, and has given full expression to the evil within himself only in his art. When Dorian dies, Wotton, the Satan-figure of *The Picture of Dorian Gray*, suffers the very terrible fate of losing his soul. In their last meeting before Dorian's suicide, Wotton speaks:

"By the way, Dorian," he said, after a pause, " 'what does it profit a man if he gain the whole world and lose —how does the quotation run?—his own soul?' "

The music jarred and Dorian Gray started, and stared at his friend. "Why do you ask me that, Harry?"

"My dear fellow," said Lord Henry, elevating his eyebrows in surprise, "I asked you because I thought you might be able to give me an answer. That is all. I was going through the Park last Sunday, and close by the Marble Arch there stood a little crowd of shabby-looking people listening to some vulgar street-preacher. As I passed by, I heard the man yelling out that question to his audience. It struck me as being rather dramatic. London is very rich in curious effects of that kind. A wet Sunday, an uncouth Christian in a mackintosh, a ring of sickly white faces under a broken roof of dripping umbrellas, and a wonderful phrase flung into the air by shrill, hysterical lips—it was really very good in its way, quite a suggestion. I thought of telling the prophet that Art had a soul, but that man had not. I am afraid, however, he would not have understood me." [*Gray*, p. 347]

What Wotton says is true primarily of himself. Lord Henry has placed his soul entirely in his art—in Dorian—and when Dorian dies he loses it. Wotton's terrible end is probably a jab at Pater, who was too timid to practice in any way what Wilde believed him to have preached.

The Picture of Dorian Gray is about the coming-of-age of Victorian art and attitudes. Wilde saw human nature in nineteenth-century England as rapidly plummeting from innocence into an awareness of the demon universe. Wotton is delighted by this. "The only people to whose opinions I listen with any respect," he says, "are people much younger than myself. They seem in front of me" (*Gray*, p. 348). Wilde's book mirrors this development, but it goes beyond that. The book contains a moral, as Wilde himself pointed out in a letter to the editor of the *St. James's Gazette:* "The moral is this: All excess, as well as all renunciation, brings its own punishment. The painter, Basil Hallward, worshipping physical beauty far too much, as most painters do, dies by the hand of one in whose soul he has created a monstrous and absurd vanity. Dorian Gray, having led a life of mere sensation and pleasure, tries to kill conscience, and at that moment kills himself. Lord Henry Wotton seeks to be merely the spectator of life. He finds that those who reject the battle are more deeply wounded than those who take part in it. Yes; there is a terrible moral in Dorian Gray" (Letters, p. 259).

Basil's attachment to the figure of Dorian—to his physical beauty and the purity it reflects—is extreme, and it destroys him, while Dorian's attempt to yield entirely to evil leads to his death. Wotton's rejection of evil in life is total, and he loses his soul but remains physically alive to endure the agonies of his spiritual damnation. What is needed, then, is a point of balance. One must neither completely renounce evil in life nor yield entirely to it. Wilde is counseling moderation in Dorian Gray: the Victorians are now deep in the demon universe, and unless they maintain a balance between good and evil, renunciation and excess, they will be destroyed.

This is true of life but not of art. In a second letter on Dorian Gray to the editor of the St. James's Gazette, Wilde wrote: "It is proper that limitations should be placed on action. It is not proper that limitations should be placed on art" (Letters, p. 261). In art, one can descend to the bottom of the demon universe and emerge unscathed. This is dramatized in the final pages of The Picture of Dorian Gray. Dorian's picture accompanies Dorian to the very depths of the demon universe, but it returns unharmed to its original state. Dorian, on the other hand, dies. The demonic, then, should be fully explored only in art, if the exploration is to remain a beautiful experience. "The artist is the creator of beautiful things," Wilde wrote in the preface to Dorian Gray, and he also wrote that "the artist can express everything." An art that delves into the dark caverns of the soul and fully explores and celebrates the evil within can remain beautiful, but a way of life that seeks fully to translate inner evil into action will finally cease to be beautiful and become an inescapable nightmare. This is Wilde's position in *The Picture of Dorian Gray,* a position he never abandoned. A biographical comment is inevitable at this point. Gone is the writer of fairy tales. Camelot is in ruins, and Wilde, now a habitual homosexual, is moving in the same direction as his protagonist, Dorian Gray. At the opening of the 1890s, Wilde was still convinced that he could escape disaster by maintaining a balance between renunciation and excess in his homosexual involvements. But in 1891 Lionel Johnson introduced him to Lord Alfred Douglas, soon to become the great passion of his life and for whose sake he was to abandon all restraint. It is fascinating that Dorian's fate prefigures Wilde's own: the novel suggests that Wilde probably had a presentiment of what the gods within had in store for him.

3 Daughters of Herodias

Lust in her naked breasts that have two eyes,
Lust in her flesh, the flesh he looks upon,
Lust that makes her whole body undulate,
Lust on her lips; the lust that never dies,
Between the hollow of her breasts, a sign
Sinister of that hell which lives within
Her limbs that long for him; her mouth like wine,
Wine that she gives to spirits more malign
Than hers.

ARTHUR SYMONS, "John and Salome"

Salome. Ah! wherefore didst thou not look at me,
Iokanaan? . . . Thou didst put upon thine eyes the covering of him who would see his God.

WILDE, *Salome*

Lady Windermere's Fan, like *The Picture of Dorian Gray,* is about the coming-of-age of Victorian England. The play, however, is a social comedy and therefore does not take us as deep into the demon universe as *Dorian Gray* did. The words *purity* and *evil,* though occasionally used by Wilde in the play, are less appropriate than the milder terms, *good* and *bad.* In discussing the theme of the fall in *Lady Windermere's Fan,* one must guard against the very serious error of imposing a dark atmosphere upon what is clearly a social comedy whose roots go as far back as Sheridan and the Restoration period. At the same time, one must recognize—and Wilde would have been delighted by the paradox—that *Lady Windermere's Fan* leads up to Wilde's blackest and most evil play, *Salome.*

The basic underlying theme of *Lady Windermere's Fan* is that modern human nature is gray: modern human beings are no longer innocent but have a large measure of badness in

73

them. The point is stressed at the very beginning of the play,
in a conversation between Lady Windermere and Lord Darlington:

> *Lady Windermere.* You think I am a Puritan, I suppose?
> Well, I have something of the Puritan in me. I was
> brought up like that. I am glad of it. My mother died
> when I was a mere child. I lived always with Lady
> Julia, my father's elder sister, you know. She was stern
> to me, but she taught me what the world is forgetting,
> the difference that there is between what is right and
> what is wrong. *She* allowed of no compromise. *I* allow
> of none.
> *Lord Darlington.* My dear Lady Windermere!
> *Lady Windermere.* (*Leaning back on the sofa.*) You look
> on me as being behind the age.—Well, I am! I should
> be sorry to be on the same level as an age like this.
> *Lord Darlington.* You think the age very bad?
> *Lady Windermere.* Yes.[1]

This is a central passage, for it states the main theme of *Lady
Windermere's Fan.* The idea of a fallen age is hit upon again
and again in the play. For instance, Lord Darlington says of
Lady Windermere: "This woman has purity and innocence.
She has everything we men have lost" (*Fan,* p. 132). Innocence
is referred to as something men once had but have lost. But
this is not only true of the men. The entire age is a fallen one,
and within respectable society, women too have forsaken goodness for gay sexual misbehavior. Here is Lady Plymdale's witty
reaction to Mrs. Erlynne, a reaction that would have horrified
Lady Windermere's Puritan aunt:

> *Lady Plymdale.* You are to lunch there on Friday!
> *Dumby.* Why?
> *Lady Plymdale.* Because I want you to take my husband
> with you. He has been so attentive lately, that he has

---

1. Oscar Wilde, *Lady Windermere's Fan,* ed. Robert Ross, pp. 8–9. All
future references to *Lady Windermere's Fan* are to this edition and are
cited in parentheses in the text. The play will be designated as *Fan.*

become a perfect nuisance. Now, this woman is just
the thing for him. He'll dance attendance upon her as
long as she lets him, and won't bother me. I assure you,
women of that kind are most useful. They form the
basis of other people's marriages. [*Fan*, p. 74]

Lady Windermere's Fan focuses on the development of Victorian England, and it is entirely appropriate that the play
should have its roots in Restoration comedy. The Restoration
era was one of colorful, witty sexual abandon following a
period of white, humorless Puritan rule. The Puritans, moreover, had closed down the theaters, but Charles II promoted
a revival of the drama. Similarly, Victorian England, with its
highly puritanical modes of conduct and its absurd melodramas, ended in fin-de-siècle corruption and a revival of the
drama that began in the 1860s, steadily gathered momentum
in the 1870s and 1880s (the plays of Gilbert, Jones, and
Pinero), and by the time of Wilde's play was poised to attain
new heights. In *Lady Windermere's Fan*, moreover, the wit of
the characters—like Wotton's—is an important measure of
their corruption.

Lord Windermere is the main exception to the trend
toward badness in the play. He is a leftover from earlier times
and is an entirely good man, though he is the target of much
vicious gossip. Dumby, reacting to the gossip about Windermere and Mrs. Erlynne, observes: "Dear Windermere is becoming almost modern. Never thought he would." But Dumby
is wrong. Windermere is not modern. For him Mrs. Erlynne
is a woman who sinned only once, many years ago, and his
desire is not to have an affair with her but to "save" her.

Lady Windermere, an avowed Puritan, is, unlike her husband, entirely good because she has not come of age: she has
not yet recognized the badness within herself. The main action
of the play takes place on the very eve of her twenty-first
birthday:

> *Lady Windermere.* You know to-day is my birthday?
> *Lord Darlington.* No? Is it really?

Lady Windermere. Yes, I'm of age to-day. Quite an important day in my life, isn't it? That is why I am giving this party to-night. [*Fan,* p. 3]

For Lady Windermere, the voice of badness is that of Lord Darlington, a voice she refuses to acknowledge in act 1 but yields to at the end of her birthday party. The superficial reason for her doing so is that she misinterprets her husband's relationship with Mrs. Erlynne, but the deeper reason is that the voice strikes a responsive chord within herself. Mrs. Erlynne triggers the response, but it comes from within Lady Windermere, who turns out to be far less of a Puritan than she had thought. Act 3 begins with her alone and cold in Lord Darlington's rooms, longing for his conversation: "He should be here. Why is he not here, to wake by passionate words some fire within me?" Lady Windermere, having come of age, finds herself poised on the very same precipice where her mother had found herself twenty years before:

Lord Windermere. Mrs. Erlynne was once honoured, loved, respected. She was well born, she had position— she lost everything—threw it away, if you like. That makes it all the more bitter. Misfortunes one can endure—they come from outside, they are accidents. But to suffer for one's own faults—ah!—there is the sting of life. It was twenty years ago, too. She was little more than a girl, then. She had been a wife for even less time than you have. [*Fan,* pp. 37–38]

It is easy to see Lady Windermere as the victim of circumstances, but this is not the case. Having come of age, she recognizes a corrupt impulse within herself and responds to it. The circumstances of her life create for her a situation where she has to make a clear choice, and she does:

Lord Darlington. Leave this house to-night. I won't tell you that the world matters nothing, or the world's voice, or the voice of society. They matter a great deal.

They matter far too much. But there are moments when one has to choose between living one's own life, fully, entirely, completely—or dragging out some false, shallow, degrading existence that the world in its hypocrisy demands. You have that moment now. Choose! Oh, my love, choose! [*Fan,* pp. 78–79]

She does choose—she makes exactly the same choice her mother had made before her.

The minute she recognizes the danger her daughter is in, Mrs. Erlynne discovers the goodness within herself. The impulse to save her child dominates her, and she takes immediate action. The task proves a difficult one, but Mrs. Erlynne succeeds, though at the expense of sacrificing her social reputation once and for all. By the end of the play, Lady Windermere has learned an important lesson about human nature: "There is the same world for all of us, and good and evil, sin and innocence, go through it hand in hand" (*Fan,* pp. 180–81).

Ironically, the lesson is not quite true. Within the Victorian period, it applies only to "modern" human nature, to human nature in the final decades of nineteenth-century Britain. It does not apply to Lord Windermere, to whom it is addressed, for he is not modern. He can worship his wife only if she remains spotless in his eyes, and Mrs. Erlynne knows this. This is why she uncompromisingly insists that her daughter never reveal to Lord Windermere what really happened in Lord Darlington's rooms. The central message of *Lady Windermere's Fan* is contained in the lengthy confrontation between Lord Windermere and Mrs. Erlynne in act 4:

> *Lord Windermere.* And as for your blunder in taking my wife's fan from here and then leaving it about in Darlington's rooms, it is unpardonable. I can't bear the sight of it now. I shall never let my wife use it again. The thing is soiled for me. You should have kept it and not brought it back.

Mrs. Erlynne. I think I *shall* keep it. (*Goes up.*) It's extremely pretty. (*Takes up fan.*) I shall ask Margaret to give it to me.

Lord Windermere. I hope my wife will give it you.

Mrs. Erlynne. Oh, I'm sure she will have no objection.

Lord Windermere. I wish that at the same time she would give you a miniature she kisses every night before she prays—It's the miniature of a young innocent-looking girl with beautiful *dark* hair.

Mrs. Erlynne. Ah, yes, I remember. How long ago that seems! (*Goes to sofa and sits down.*) It was done before I was married. Dark hair and an innocent expression were the fashion then, Windermere. [*Fan,* pp. 163–65]

Just as the fan has become for Lord Windermere a symbol of corruption, the miniature his wife kisses every night is a symbol of total spiritual purity. Mrs. Erlynne, moreover, points out that the innocent-looking, dark-haired miniature of her Lord Windermere so much admires was the *fashion* when she was a young girl—that is, in the late sixties and early seventies. In graphic art, the dominant figure of that period was Dante Gabriel Rossetti. His model during the time was Jane Morris, a beautiful, innocent-looking young girl with dark hair (his early model, the blonde Elizabeth Siddal, died in 1862). Rossetti's innocent ladies were erotic symbols of utter spiritual purity. The Victorians of the time—"How long ago that seems!"—were attracted to such paintings of Rossetti's because their souls were still largely within the protective shell of innocence and they were fascinated by the ideal of purity. The age has developed a new, more mature soul, however, and now painted women with dyed hair, a knowing expression, and shapely figures are the ones who enchant the men. Cecil Graham, who seems somewhat ahead of the others in his corruption, considers good women unbearable but finds that Mrs. Erlynne can exercise a strange power over him:

Dumby. (*To Cecil Graham.*) Did you introduce Mrs. Erlynne to Lady Jedburgh?

Cecil Graham. Had to, my dear fellow. Couldn't help it! That woman can make one do anything she wants. How, I don't know. [*Fan,* p. 69]

Mrs. Erlynne understands the age, and she knows that both Lord and Lady Windermere must be shielded from some of its truths if their marriage is to survive. Under no circumstances must Lady Windermere discover who her real mother is— the idea of a pure, dead mother to be adored and emulated must be preserved if she is to remain sufficiently virtuous for her husband. The influence a beloved mother can exert upon her daughter's development is great, even if the mother is dead. (This is comically underlined by the relationship between the duchess of Berwick and her daughter, Lady Agatha. The daughter's one line in the play is "Yes, mama," repeated over and over again.) Mrs. Erlynne also knows what social ostracism is like, and will go to any lengths to save her daughter from it. When Windermere declares he is going to tell his wife who her mother really is, Mrs. Erlynne's response is savage: "If you do, I will make my name so infamous that it will mar every moment of her life. It will ruin her, and make her wretched. If you dare to tell her, there is no depth of degradation I will not sink to, no pit of shame I will not enter. You shall not tell her—I forbid you" (*Fan,* p. 169).

One of the paradoxes of *Lady Windermere's Fan* is that Mrs. Erlynne is far more modern than her daughter. The daughter continues to cling to the past, worshiping a dead, virtuous mother, while the mother takes the modern road. She says to the horrified Windermere: "What consoles one nowadays is not repentance, but pleasure. Repentance is quite out of date" (*Fan,* p. 167). Her maternal feelings had proved too painful, and she decides that she does not wish to experience them again. Being bad, she finds, is far more comfortable than being good.

Mrs. Erlynne is not exactly a daughter of Herodias—she is not entirely bad—but she is certainly a far cry from the blessed damozels Rossetti worshiped. The evolution from

Lady Windermere's supposedly dead mother to Lady Windermere to Mrs. Erlynne reflects the evolution of the age. Within
the social-comedy framework, however, it is also a considerable
step toward the vampire woman, and in this respect the play
introduces to *Salome,* where the evil in human nature, of
which Salome is the concentrated symbol, shatters all molds
and engulfs everything.

Salome is Wilde's most symbolic and least understood play.
It conforms fully to its author's idea that symbolism should
be "many-sided" and "suggestive of many meanings." [2]—which
is very different from saying, of course, that its symbols can
mean anything. Intended for an English audience but origi-
nally written and published in French, *Salome* was translated
into English by Lord Alfred Douglas. The translation was
either totally rejected or drastically revised by Wilde himself,
who was highly displeased with Douglas's version, and who
also rejected a subsequent rendering by Beardsley. When the
play first appeared in English, it did not bear Douglas's name
on the title page as translator, but read simply: "Translated
from the French of Oscar Wilde." Wilde pacified his friend,
though, by dedicating the play to him and naming him as
translator in the dedication. Subsequently, however—in the
1931 edition of his *Autobiography*—Douglas admitted that the
published translation was Wilde's, not his, or at least was so
altered as to bear little or no resemblance to his version.[3]

For the English-speaking world, *Salome* has always existed
as the English *Salome,* and there is a very good reason why
the English version of the play should have priority over the
French. Wilde's French, though good, was not excellent. It is

2. See *Letters,* p. 315. Wilde praises a tale by Coulson Kernahan because its symbolism is "suggestive of many meanings, not narrowed down
to one moral, but many-sided as, I think, symbolism should be."
3. Holbrook Jackson, introduction to Oscar Wilde, *Salome* (New York:
Heritage Press, 1945), pp. 4–15. See especially p. 11. Jackson, in the introduction, discusses at some length the question of who translated *Salome,*
and concludes—albeit hesitantly—that it was Wilde himself.

possible that André Gide helped him while he was writing the
French version, and definite that Marcel Schwob made corrections in it after it was completed. The French *Salome* was also
submitted to Pierre Louÿs for corrections. It may be said, then,
that Wilde was not the final authority in deciding the ultimate nature of the French *Salome*—a statement that cannot
be made about the English version of the play.

A brief comparison of the two *Salome*'s will show that the
English version is almost a literal translation of the French;
but there is more to the matter than that. Holbrook Jackson
has written about the English *Salome:* "It was not the mere
rendering of words from one language to another that was
required. The French of the original is so simple and direct
that a literal translation was almost inevitable. The difficulty
was with texture and *cadence.*" [4] Indeed, *Salome* is a play
that aspires toward the condition of music, and that was
turned into a very successful opera by Richard Strauss. Wilde
must surely have wanted the words, phrases, and sentences of
Salome to fuse in total harmony, without a single discordant
note to disturb the play's rhythmic flow. Under these circumstances, translation becomes creation. The result is such a
brilliant success that one can only heartily believe Douglas
when he asserts that the English *Salome* was composed by
Wilde. Only an artist of the highest caliber could have produced such a stunning effect, and Douglas was no such thing.
If, then, the English *Salome* is Wilde's and the French version
was touched by Schwob and Louÿs, and perhaps also Gide, it
is best to turn to the English version as the more reliable one
—the *Salome* that is more purely Oscar Wilde's. In my analysis
of *Salome,* therefore, I shall use the English version throughout.

The play opens with two opposing views of Salome, one
angelic and the other demonic:

> *The Young Syrian.* How beautiful is the Princess Salome
> to-night!

4. Ibid., p. 11. Italics mine.

The Page of Herodias. Look at the moon. How strange
the moon seems! She is like a woman rising from a
tomb. She is like a dead woman. One might fancy
she was looking for dead things.
The Young Syrian. She has a strange look. She is like a
little princess who wears a yellow veil, and whose feet
are of silver. She is like a princess who has little white
doves for feet. One might fancy she was dancing.
The Page of Herodias. She is like a woman who is dead.[5]

The thrust of the play is to strip veil after veil from Salome
until she emerges as a deathly pale terror feeding on the
blood-soaked head of a dead person. The demonic vision is
entirely confirmed, the angelic vision entirely refuted.

The setting of the play is a feast, an orgy of eating and
drinking with heavy sexual overtones. We first meet Salome
when she emerges into the night air, in an apparently angelic
rejection of the sin-tainted feast:

Salome. I will not stay. I cannot stay. Why does the
Tetrarch look at me all the while with his mole's eye
under his shaking eyelids? It is strange that the hus-
band of my mother looks at me like that. I know not
what it means. Of a truth I know it too well.
The Young Syrian. You have left the feast, Princess?
Salome. How sweet is the air here! I can breathe here.
[*Salome,* p. 10]

Salome's behavior at this point is that of a spotless virgin. The
opening lines of the play identified her inextricably with the
moon, and she now deepens the identification:

Salome. How good to see the moon! She is like a little
piece of money, a little silver flower. She is cold and
chaste. I am sure she is a virgin. She has the beauty of

5. Oscar Wilde, *Salome* (London: Elkin Mathews and John Lane, and
Boston: Copeland and Day, 1894), pp. 1–2. All future references to *Salome*
are to this edition and are cited in parentheses in the text. The play will
be designated as *Salome.*

a virgin. Yes, she is a virgin. She has never defiled herself. She has never abandoned herself to men, like the other goddesses. [*Salome*, p. 11]

It soon becomes apparent, however, that Salome has rejected Herod's feast because she wants a feast of a different nature. What Salome wants is to feed on a dead thing—on a lover so sterile and deathlike that he can pose no threat whatsoever to her virginity. Iokanaan is Salome's natural choice for a lover, and what first attracts her to him is his voice denouncing the lust and abandon of Herod and Herodias and conveniently declaring that his rod is broken. The voice suggests a sterile and death-oriented nature, and Salome orders Iokanaan released from his prison. This is her reaction to him when he emerges:

> *Salome.* Ah, but he is terrible, he is terrible!
> *The Young Syrian.* Do not stay here, Princess, I beseech you.
> *Salome.* It is his eyes above all that are terrible. They are like black holes burned by torches in a tapestry of Tyre. They are like the black caverns where the dragons live, the black caverns of Egypt in which the dragons make their lairs. They are like black lakes troubled by fantastic moons. . . . Do you think he will speak again?
> *The Young Syrian.* Do not stay here, Princess. I pray you do not stay here.
> *Salome.* How wasted he is! He is like a thin ivory statue. He is like an image of silver. I am sure he is chaste, as the moon is. He is like a moonbeam, like a shaft of silver. His flesh must be very cold, cold as ivory. . . . I would look closer at him. [*Salome*, p. 19]

The passage is worthy of close analysis—as, indeed, every passage in *Salome* is. Salome is fascinated by a deathlike quality in Iokanaan. Earlier, when she had looked into Iokanaan's prison, she had said: "How black it is, down there! It must be

terrible to be in so black a hole! It is like a tomb" (*Salome,*
p. 15). Black is the color of death, and Salome describes the
prophet's eyes as "black holes," then as "black caverns," and
finally as "black lakes." Holes, caverns, and lakes, moreover,
all suggest depth—the black depth of the tomb. She then
shifts to white, which is the color of chastity or sterility but
also suggests the pallor of a corpse. She associates Iokanaan
with cold and lifeless art objects—ivory statues, silver images—
and it is the deathlike coldness of his flesh that attracts her.
By identifying Iokanaan with the moon, moreover, Salome
claims him for her own, since she and the moon at the
beginning of the play form a union that is never dissolved.

The moon symbolism of *Salome* is of crucial importance.
As the play progresses, it becomes increasingly apparent that
the moon is meant to suggest the terrible pagan goddess
Cybele. Cybele in mythology is the symbol of the aggressive,
sexually perverse female whose sterile sex impulse is directed
toward the subjugation and castration of the male. As
different cultures adopted the worship of Cybele, these savage
characteristics of the goddess were gradually refined away
until the Greeks eventually confused or identified her with
Aphrodite.

Cybele was a virgin with eunuch priests who regularly
castrated themselves on entering her service. The hallmarks
of the cruel goddess are the tremendous value she places on
her virginity, her obsessive and perverse preoccupation with
male sexuality, and her love for the holy king Attis. Sir James
Frazer, in *The Golden Bough; A Study in Magic and Religion,* which first appeared in two volumes in 1890, writes
about the death of Attis: "Two different accounts of the death
of Attis were current. According to the one he was killed by a
boar, like Adonis. According to the other he unmanned himself under a pine tree, and bled to death on the spot. The
latter is said to have been the local story told by the people
of Pessinus, a great seat of the worship of Cybele, and the
whole legend of which the story forms a part is stamped with
a character of rudeness and savagery which speaks strongly for

its antiquity." [6] The most savage version of the second account is that Cybele herself destroyed Attis by tearing out his sexual organs after he had mated with her on a mountaintop. It is with this goddess that Salome blends in the play, though the two remain distinguishable. Cybele is pure essence—as the moon, she is eternal and nightly bathes the whole world in her rays—while Salome is that essence captured for a moment in time. The play is dominated by a full and clear moon, and all the arguments and confusion about religion take place under the gaze of that moon. Cybele is the only true divinity, the light of the world, and she reveals herself to all who wish to see. Christ never appears in the play, and, ironically, it is Salome who fulfills Iokanaan's ambiguous prophecies. It is through her, not through Christ, that the true God revealed Himself—or rather Herself—on earth in biblical times; and it is she, not Christ, whom Wilde presents as the incarnate God. "Behold the time is come!" cries Iokanaan a few minutes before Salome's dance. "That which I foretold has come to pass. The day that I spake of is at hand" (*Salome*, p. 33).

But what comes is Salome, who dances the dance of the seven veils, and it is because of her, not because of the Crucifixion, that the moon becomes like blood and the kings of the earth grow afraid. Iokanaan is indeed a prophet, but a blind one who does not understand what he is prophesying. He speaks of Christ, of the arrival of the true divinity, and the true divinity does arrive, only it is not Christ. I shall give a full interpretation of Iokanaan later on, but what should be

6. Sir James Frazer, *The Golden Bough; A Study in Magic and Religion*, abridged ed. (London: Macmillan, 1922), p. 347. I have been unable to ascertain whether the section on Cybele appears in the original 1890 edition of *The Golden Bough*, but if—as I strongly suspect—it does, this should historically substantiate my reading of *Salome* in terms of the worship of Cybele. At any rate, I do not propose in this book to trace Wilde's sources concerning Cybele. It is definitely arguable, however, that *The Golden Bough* was at least a secondary influence on Wilde, for it promoted a great deal of interest in mythology, magic, and pagan Oriental religions at the time of its first publication in 1890.

clear now is that he, without knowing it, is the mouthpiece
of Cybele, and he correctly prophesies an evil Apocalypse in
which everything explodes in terror and total lust. "In that
day the sun shall become black like sackcloth of hair," he
cries, "and the moon shall become like blood, and the stars
of the heaven shall fall upon the earth like unripe figs that
fall from the fig-tree, and the kings of the earth shall be
afraid" (Salome, p. 44).

It is Apocalypse that Iokanaan is prophesying, and it is precisely with an evil Apocalypse that the play ends. The moon
does become blood-red, Salome indulges in an unrestrained
orgy of sterile lust, the Tetrarch's fear springs into the open,
and a midnight blackness finally engulfs everything. Salome
is a highly religious play, but its religion is entirely demonic—
a religion of evil. Wilde's treatment of demonism in this play
is wholly original. No other author writing in English before
him had ever celebrated demonism as a true religion.
Beardsley, moreover, was very alive to the evil religious content of Salome, and in his title-page illustration—reproduced
elsewhere in this book—he painted a smiling, clearly Satanic,
naked Salome flanked by huge candles, with a nude demon-
angel, a knowing smile on its face, bowed in a position of worship before her.

That the moon is meant to suggest Cybele becomes relatively clear in the episode of the young Syrian's death, for
his main function in the play is to worship Salome in the
same way that Cybele was worshiped by her inferior clergy.
The worship of Cybele is compactly described by Frazer in
one of the most compelling passages of The Golden Bough:

> The third day, the twenty-fourth of March, was known
> as the Day of Blood: the Archigallus or high-priest drew
> blood from his arms and presented it as an offering.
> Nor was he alone in making this bloody sacrifice. Stirred
> by the wild barbaric music of clashing cymbals, rumbling
> drums, droning horns, and screaming flutes, the inferior
> clergy whirled about in the dance with waggling heads

and streaming hair, until, rapt into a frenzy of excitement and insensible to pain, they gashed their bodies with potsherds or slashed them with knives in order to bespatter the altar and the sacred tree with their flowing blood. The ghastly rite probably formed part of the mourning for Attis and may have been intended to strengthen him for the resurrection. . . . Further, we may conjecture, though we are not expressly told, that it was on the same Day of Blood and for the same purpose that the novices sacrificed their virility. Wrought to the highest pitch of religious excitement they dashed the severed portions of themselves against the image of the cruel goddess.[7]

The death of the young Syrian closely parallels the behavior of the novices and inferior clergy on the Day of Blood. He is obviously under Salome's spell from the beginning of the play, and she uses her sexual charms to bring him to a high pitch of excitement and render him helpless under her control:

> *Salome.* Thou wilt do this thing for me, Narraboth, and to-morrow when I pass in my litter beneath the gateway of the idol-sellers I will let fall for thee a little flower, a little green flower.
> *The Young Syrian.* Princess, I cannot, I cannot.
> *Salome. (Smiling.)* Thou wilt do this thing for me, Narraboth. Thou knowest that thou wilt do this thing for me. And on the morrow when I shall pass in my litter by the bridge of the idol-buyers, I will look at thee through the muslin veils, I will look at thee, Narraboth, it may be I will smile at thee. Look at me, Narraboth, look at me. Ah! thou knowest that thou wilt do what I ask of thee. Thou knowest it. . . . I know that thou wilt do this thing.

7. Ibid., p. 349.

> *The Young Syrian. (Signing to the third Soldier.)* Let the
> prophet come forth. . . . The Princess Salome desires
> to see him. [*Salome,* pp. 16–17]

Salome forces the young Syrian to bring Iokanaan to her,
and then to spill his blood as a sacrifice to Iokanaan, in a final
effort to make the prophet respond positively to her wooing.
The young Syrian is also sacrificed, however, to protect
Salome's virginity, thereby establishing an ambivalence similar to the ambivalence of the orgies of the Day of Blood,
where the self-mutilation with knives and the cutting out of
male sexual organs, though intended to resurrect Attis, also
satisfied Cybele's desire to castrate and subjugate the male.
Here is how the young Syrian dies:

> *Salome.* I will kiss thy mouth, Iokanaan. I will kiss thy
> mouth.
> *The Young Syrian.* Princess, Princess, thou who art like
> a garden of myrrh, thou who art the dove of all doves,
> look not at this man, look not at him! Do not speak
> such words to him. I cannot endure it. . . . Princess,
> do not speak these things.
> *Salome.* I will kiss thy mouth, Iokanaan.
> *The Young Syrian.* Ah! (*He kills himself, and falls be-
> tween Salome and Iokanaan.*) [*Salome,* p. 24]

Though it is not explicitly stated, it is fair to assume that the
young Syrian used a knife or a sword to kill himself, for he
is a captain of the guard and these were the weapons of the
day. A knife or a sword is an obvious phallic symbol, and the
young Syrian is wrought up by Salome to the highest pitch
of sexual excitement, then pushed to turn his male sexuality
against himself by destroying himself. Salome remains as aloof
as Cybele's lifeless image while this occurs, but the page of
Herodias sees it as deliberate murder:

> *The Page of Herodias.* Well I knew that the moon was
> seeking a dead thing, but I knew not that it was he
> whom she sought. Ah! Why did I not hide him from

the moon? If I had hidden him in a cavern she would not have seen him. [*Salome,* p. 25]

Cybele rendered up her virginity for the holy king Attis, and Salome's identification with Cybele deepens when she symbolically renders up her virginity for Iokanaan. This change in Salome is mirrored in the moon:

> *Herod.* The moon has a strange look to-night. Has she not a strange look? She is like a mad woman, a mad woman who is seeking everywhere for lovers. She is naked too. She is quite naked. The clouds are seeking to clothe her nakedness, but she will not let them. She shows herself naked in the sky. She reels through the clouds like a drunken woman. . . . I am sure she is looking for lovers. Does she not reel like a drunken woman? She is like a mad woman, is she not? [*Salome,* pp. 27–28]

Cybele murdered Attis for robbing her of her virginity, and this is one reason why Salome's love for Iokanaan is from the beginning colored by hate and why she asks for his head in the end. As she holds the severed head, she says to it: "I was a virgin, and thou didst take my virginity from me. I was chaste, and thou didst fill my veins with fire" (*Salome,* p. 65). Though she remains physically a virgin to the end, on the symbolic level Salome yields her virginity to Iokanaan in the play. Cybele tore out Attis's sexual organs in revenge, but Salome dispenses with Iokanaan's entire body.

Salome's wooing of Iokanaan is extremely important and should be analyzed in great detail. It is marked by an ambivalence that becomes more pronounced with each successive rejection. Here is Salome's first approach to him:

> *Salome.* I am amorous of thy body, Iokanaan! Thy body is white, like the lilies of a field that the mower hath never mowed. Thy body is white like the snows that lie on the mountains of Judæa, and come down into the valleys. The roses in the garden of the Queen of

Arabia are not so white as thy body. Neither the roses
of the garden of the Queen of Arabia, the garden of
spices of the Queen of Arabia, nor the feet of the dawn
when they light on the leaves, nor the breast of the
moon when she lies on the breast of the sea. [*Salome*,
pp. 21–22]

Salome finds Iokanaan's body beautiful because of its white-
ness, but the color white suggests a cold lifelessness, and this is
made explicit by its identification with snow. In other words,
it is Iokanaan's sterility that Salome is attracted to. One can
be absolutely positive of the sterility only of dead men, however, and Salome betrays a slight fear of Iokanaan when she
compares him to the dawn, since the dawn brings the sun and
obscures the moon. Salome's desire to destroy Iokanaan is
suggested by the suppressed ominousness of the first simile.
The lilies in the field may never have been mowed, but the
suggestion of a mower is disturbing.

After she is rejected, Salome's hatred of Iokanaan explodes,
but she soon puts it aside and approaches the prophet a
second time:

Salome. It is of thy hair that I am enamoured, Iokanaan.
Thy hair is like clusters of grapes, like the clusters of
black grapes that hang from the vine-trees of Edom
in the land of the Edomites. Thy hair is like the cedars
of Lebanon, like the great cedars of Lebanon that give
their shade to the lions and to the robbers who would
hide them by day. The long black nights, when the
moon hides her face, when the stars are afraid, are not
so black as thy hair. The silence that dwells in the
forest is not so black. There is nothing in the world
that is so black as thy hair. [*Salome*, pp. 22–23]

Again, it is a deathlike, sterile quality in Iokanaan that attracts Salome. Black is the color of death, and it holds Salome
spellbound. The feast imagery here should also be noted.
Iokanaan's hair is compared to delicious black grapes that

Salome wishes to feast on. Salome, however, has deep reservations about Iokanaan, for she sees his blackness as hiding the face of the moon. After Iokanaan's second rejection of her, Salome realizes that if she wishes to possess and control the prophet, she will have to kill him. Her third approach to Iokanaan clearly suggests that she has chosen to sacrifice him on the altar of her lust:

> *Salome.* It is thy mouth that I desire, Iokanaan. Thy mouth is like a band of scarlet on a tower of ivory. It is like a pomegranate cut in twain with a knife of ivory. The pomegranate flowers that blossom in the gardens of Tyre, and are redder than roses, are not so red. The red blasts of trumpets that herald the approach of kings, and make afraid the enemy, are not so red. Thy mouth is redder than the feet of those who tread the wine in the wine-press. It is redder than the feet of the doves who inhabit the temples and are fed by the priests. It is redder than the feet of him who cometh from a forest where he hath slain a lion, and seen gilded tigers. [*Salome*, p. 23]

Again, we have feast imagery—Iokanaan's mouth is compared to a ripe pomegranate. Again, what attracts Salome to Iokanaan is a deathlike quality in him—red is the color of blood and is overtly identified with blood. What is new is the sacrificial imagery. The redness of Iokanaan's mouth is associated with the blood that flows on the sacrificial altars of the priests. Knives and the slaying of lions are mentioned, and the comparison of Iokanaan's mouth to a pomegranate cut in half with a knife is sinister. That the knife is made of ivory is even more sinister, for an ivory knife suggests a sacrificial knife and is related to priests and altars. Salome's true nature is rapidly unveiling itself.

The last veils obscuring Salome's nature fall after she dances the dance of the seven veils and receives Iokanaan's head for her reward. Her final, lengthy address to Iokanaan as she metaphorically feasts on his blood-soaked head is full of many meanings, but it is conspicuous for its lack of ambivalence. All hatred of Iokanaan is gone, for he is now totally sterile and totally under Salome's control. She can do whatever she wishes with his head now, even throw it to the dogs. But she will not throw it to the dogs, for a very simple reason: "I love thee yet, Iokanaan. I love only thee. . . . I am athirst for thy beauty; I am hungry for thy body; and neither wine nor apples can appease my desire. What shall I do now, Iokanaan? Neither the floods nor the great waters can quench my passion" (*Salome,* p. 65). The only thing for her to do is to feast insatiably on the head: "Ah! Thou wouldst not suffer me to kiss thy mouth, Iokanaan. Well! I will kiss it now. I will bite it with my teeth as one bites a ripe fruit. Yes, I will kiss thy mouth, Iokanaan" (*Salome,* p. 64). And the "feast" continues until the horrified Herod puts an end to it.

If Wilde were portraying Salome simply as an individual, this play would have little intellectual depth. Salome, however, is presented as a symbol of human nature, entirely evil because entirely uninhibited and unmodified by any restrictions. Wilde's vision of human nature in *Salome* is not very different from Conrad's in *Heart of Darkness,* though the attitude of the two writers toward evil differs. Salome, like Pater's Mona Lisa, looms as a symbol of human nature, but she is a symbol that has shattered and destroyed the mold of the Mona Lisa. Pater identified the Mona Lisa with the vampire, who "has been dead many times, and learned the secrets of the grave," but he also identified her with Saint Anne, the mother of Mary. Salome, on the other hand, is simply a lustful vampire, an unholy terror.

The Romantics and Rossetti had seriously attempted to explore the depths of the human soul and had confronted the demonic in human nature. Pater, in *The Renaissance,* had seen modern human nature as heavily streaked with evil, and had been fascinated by the Satanic element in it. Wilde in *Salome,* however, was the first person to view the human soul as entirely evil and—in contrast to Pater—to delve into the ancient and mythic past of the race to find the baldest, most unrestrained expressions of this evil. In *Salome,* moreover, Satanism is far more overt than in *The Renaissance:* it shatters all molds and restrictions and is elevated to the status of a religion.

It should also be mentioned here that Wilde, in his presentation of Salome, was probably influenced by Huysmans's *A Rebours.* Des Esseintes had been held spellbound by Gustave Moreau's oil painting of Salome. For him, an irresistible fascination breathed from Moreau's canvas, and he saw Salome not merely as an individual but as the symbolic incarnation of world-old Vice, a poisonous goddess of Accursed Beauty. In Moreau's watercolor, "The Apparition," Salome appeared to Des Esseintes as being less majestic and imposing than ensnaring to the senses, capable of awakening the sleeping passions of man with her unholy charm. For him, a hypnotizing, demonic aura radiated from both paintings. Quite probably, the Salome passages in *A Rebours* were at least partly responsible for firing Wilde's imagination to create his masterpiece of the decadent movement.

That Salome is meant to represent human nature is made clear in the play, for Wilde offers no alternative to her except repression, no final escape from her except death. She is the ultimate and only reality, and not to recognize this is a form of blindness. Great stress is laid in the play on sight, on looking and seeing. The idea that one can discover the perfect manifestation of his soul in the outside world is a prominent one in Wilde. In *Salome,* Salome is the perfect visible symbol of the human soul, which is now no longer "gray" but entirely evil. This vision of the soul, however, is so terrible that human beings deliberately blind themselves in varying degrees to escape its full impact and horror. Symbolically speaking, Iokanaan never looks at Salome, and she ultimately says to his severed head: "Lift up thine eyelids, Iokanaan! Wherefore dost thou not look at me? Art thou afraid of me, Iokanaan, that thou wilt not look at me?" (*Salome,* p. 64). Herod, who looks at Salome too much, knows what he is looking at, and grows progressively more afraid: "It is true, I have looked at thee and ceased not this night. Thy beauty has troubled me. Thy beauty has grievously troubled me, and I have looked at thee overmuch. Nay, but I will look at thee no more. One should not look at anything. Neither at things, nor at people should one look. Only in mirrors is it well to look, for mirrors do but show us masks" (*Salome*, p. 58). A mirror will show Herod a mask, but Salome reveals his soul to him.

The blindest person in the play, however, is Iokanaan, who has savagely repressed the evil in himself. Salome says to the head, whose eyes have been forever closed: "Ah! wherefore didst thou not look at me, Iokanaan? With the cloak of thine hands, and with the cloak of thy blasphemies thou didst hide thy face. Thou didst put upon thine eyes the covering of him who would see his God. Well, thou has seen thy God, Iokanaan, but me, me, thou didst never see. If thou hadst seen me thou hadst loved me" (*Salome*, p. 65). Had Iokanaan looked at Salome, he would have seen the perfect embodiment of his soul, and would have fallen in love. But Iokanaan, from the beginning of the play, is totally blind: he has thrust the evil and lust in himself into his subconscious. This is one reason why he dwells in the total blackness of a tomblike cistern. "I will not look at thee," he informs Salome, then returns to the black cistern she had released him from. Salome, on the other hand, dwells in the clear moonlight, for she refuses to hide her nature and repress her lust.

Human nature, however, though it can be repressed, cannot be eliminated. Iokanaan is a fascinating study. It is as a disembodied voice that we first meet him, and his words continually betray the lust and evil that he has hidden from himself. When Salome first hears his voice, these are his words:

> *The Voice of Iokanaan.* Behold! the Lord hath come. The Son of Man is at hand. The centaurs have hidden themselves in the rivers, and the nymphs have left the rivers, and are lying beneath the leaves in the forests. [*Salome*, p. 11]

What Iokanaan is saying, on the conscious level, is that the coming of Christ has swept away pagan concepts. Centaurs and nymphs, however, are sexual creatures, and Christ's coming has the effect of making them hide themselves. On the subconscious level, what Iokanaan is saying is that Christ's advent has thrust the sexual impulse into the dark recesses of the mind and forced it to hide itself from view. This kind of double entendre characterizes much of what Iokanaan says in the play. The lust within him constantly asserts itself in his words without his becoming conscious of it. Certainly, the sexual imagery inherent in a passage such as the following is unmistakable:

> *The Voice of Iokanaan.* Rejoice not, O land of Palestine, because the rod of him who smote thee is broken. For from the seed of the serpent shall come a basilisk, and that which is born of it shall devour the birds. [*Salome,* p. 13]

To understand Iokanaan, it is best to begin by examining his relationship to Herod and Herodias. Iokanaan and Herod in the play are presented as mirror opposites, and there is in each a sufficient amount of the other to suggest their kinship. Iokanaan is Herod's conscience, and his untiring condemnation of Herod's incestuous relationship with Herodias finds a response within the Tetrarch. The kinship of the two men is stressed by the fact that they seem at times to share the same intuitive consciousness. Iokanaan says to Salome:

> *Iokanaan.* Art thou not afraid, daughter of Herodias? Did I not tell thee that I had heard in the palace the beating of the wings of the angel of death, and hath he not come, the angel of death? [*Salome,* p. 25]

Very soon afterward, Herod has the following conversation with his wife:

> *Herod.* It is cold here. There is a wind blowing. Is there not a wind blowing?

Herodias. No; there is no wind.

Herod. I tell you there is a wind that blows. . . . And I
hear in the air something that is like the beating of
wings, like the beating of vast wings. Do you not
hear it?

Herodias. I hear nothing.

Herod. I hear it no longer. But I heard it. It was the
blowing of the wind. It has passed away. But no, I
hear it again. Do you not hear it? It is just like a
beating of wings. [*Salome,* p. 31]

The mind of Iokanaan and that of Herod show a remarkable receptivity to each other in these passages, indicating
that the two men are really one man split in half.

It is clear in the play, moreover, that the lustful Herod,
a murderer sated with forbidden pleasures, has a tendency
to react against the evil in himself. This is made manifest
by his interest in Christ and his fear of Iokanaan. Consider
the following quotation:

Herodias. I do not believe in prophets. Can a man tell
what will come to pass? No man knows it. Also he is
for ever insulting me. But I think you are afraid of
him. . . . I know well that you are afraid of him.

Herod. I am not afraid of him. I am afraid of no man.

Herodias. I tell you you are afraid of him. If you are
not afraid of him why do you not deliver him to the
Jews who for these six months past have been clamoring
for him?

A Jew. Truly, my lord, it were better to deliver him into
our hands.

Herod. Enough on this subject. I have already given you
my answer. I will not deliver him into your hands. He
is a holy man. He is a man who has seen God. [*Salome,*
p. 34]

Herod calls Iokanaan a holy man who has seen God, but he
imprisons him in a black, tomblike underground cistern and

forbids anyone to let him out or even to talk to him. The symbolism of this is apparent: the cistern suggests Herod's subconscious mind, in which he has suppressed one aspect of his nature in an attempt to get rid of it. This attempt has not been wholly successful, however, for to repress is not to abolish. Iokanaan remains alive, both physically and within Herod. Herod is mostly unaware of the Iokanaan within himself and denies that he is affected by the prophet's words, but his fear manifests itself nevertheless and is quite apparent to Herodias and Salome. A good example of Herod's fear of Iokanaan can be seen in his reaction to the news that Christ raises the dead:

> *Herod.* I do not wish Him to do that. I forbid Him to do that. I suffer no man to raise the dead. This Man must be found and told that I forbid Him to raise the dead. [*Salome,* p. 40]

If we remember that Herod has, in effect, imprisoned Iokanaan in a tomb, then his fear of Iokanaan becomes very apparent.

Just as Herod has been unable to eliminate the Iokanaan in himself, Iokanaan has been unable to eliminate the Herod within himself. At the beginning of *Salome,* Iokanaan, in a lengthy passage, is implicitly identified with Herodias's first husband:

> *The Cappadocian. (Pointing to the cistern.)* What a strange prison!
> *Second Soldier.* It is an old cistern.
> *The Cappadocian.* An old cistern! That must be a poisonous place in which to dwell!
> *Second Soldier.* Oh no! For instance, the Tetrarch's brother, his elder brother, the first husband of Herodias the Queen, was imprisoned there for twelve years. It did not kill him. At the end of the twelve years he had to be strangled.
> *The Cappadocian.* Strangled? Who dared to do that?

Second Soldier. (Pointing to the Executioner, a huge negro.) That man yonder, Naaman.
The Cappadocian. He was not afraid?
Second Soldier. Oh no! The Tetrarch sent him the ring.
The Cappadocian. What ring?
Second Soldier. The death ring. So he was not afraid.
The Cappadocian. Yet it is a terrible thing to strangle a king. [*Salome,* pp. 8–9]

There are several points of similarity between Herodias's first husband and Iokanaan. They both shared the same prison. Moreover, Herodias's first husband held a highly elevated position—he was king—and Iokanaan holds a highly elevated position—he is a prophet. Looking ahead, Iokanaan, too, is executed by order of Herod and by the same executioner who killed Herodias's first husband.

The passage is undoubtedly meant to foreshadow Iokanaan's death, but it also lends an added significance to the prophet's sustained verbal attack on Herod and Herodias, for it darkly suggests that Iokanaan is Herodias's lover at one remove. On the conscious level, the prophet's attack is motivated by genuine moral indignation. There is, however, another, entirely unconscious, reason for his attack—Iokanaan wants Herodias for himself and wishes to wrest her away from Herod. What Herod has consciously desired and obtained, Iokanaan subconsciously desires. His attack on Herodias is heavily charged with sexual references:

Iokanaan. Where is she who gave herself unto the Captains of Assyria, who have baldricks on their loins, and crowns of many colours on their heads? Where is she who hath given herself to the young men of the Egyptians, who are clothed in fine linen and hyacinth, whose shields are of gold, whose helmets are of silver, whose bodies are mighty? Go, bid her rise up from the bed of her abominations, from the bed of her incestuousness, that she may hear the words of him who prepareth the way of the Lord, that she may repent of her iniquities.

Though she will not repent, but will stick fast in her
abominations, go bid her come. [*Salome*, p. 18]

This is a fascinating passage, for Iokanaan, without being
conscious of it, is reaching out for the very woman he is
condemning: he wants his share of Herodias, and is calling
upon her to rise up from the bed of her abominations and
come to him, *though she will not repent*. The passage is a
masterpiece of double entendre, a subtle revelation of the lust
that lurks hidden within Iokanaan.

Herodias, however, is an older and less physically attractive
version of Salome. She is Salome's mother, she is sexually
perverse like Salome, and she fully approves of Salome's
desire to destroy Iokanaan. The two women are sexual rivals,
though, and Salome is the ultimate victor. Herod, tired of his
wife, consciously and lustfully begins to concentrate his at-
tentions on her daughter. On the same night, the same thing
begins to occur in Iokanaan on the subconscious level.

Iokanaan's shift from Herodias to Salome is indicated in
the structural movement of the play, for he begins to turn his
attention to Salome almost immediately after his above-
quoted address to Herodias. It is evident, moreover, from his
initial reaction to Salome that he is strongly attracted to her:

> *Iokanaan.* Who is this woman who is looking at me? I
> will not have her look at me. Wherefore doth she look
> at me, with her golden eyes, under her gilded eyelids?
> I know not who she is. I do not desire to know who
> she is. Bid her begone. [*Salome*, p. 20]

The mere gaze of Salome sends a shock through Iokanaan,
and the panicky vehemence with which he insists that he does
not wish to know who she is betrays him by its very intensity.
As she approaches him, he shrinks from her and cries: "Back!
daughter of Babylon! Come not near the chosen of the Lord."
As Salome woos him, his repeated rejections of her are so
exaggeratedly violent as to suggest a great fear of her, a
tremendous effort to prevent his repressed longing for her

from erupting forth into the open. He succeeds, Salome is
rejected, and Iokanaan voluntarily withdraws into his tomblike prison, preferring blindness to acknowledging his soul.
His desire for Salome remains repressed, lurking in his subconscious, destined never to see the light.

It emerges in his words, however. Here is Iokanaan after his
confrontation with Salome is over and he is safely back in his
cistern:

> *The Voice of Iokanaan.* Ah! the wanton one! The harlot!
> Ah! the daughter of Babylon with her golden eyes and
> her gilded eyelids! Thus saith the Lord God, Let there
> come up against her a multitude of men. Let the people
> take stones and stone her. . . .
>
> *Herodias.* Command him to be silent!
>
> *The Voice of Iokanaan.* Let the captains of the hosts
> pierce her with their swords, let them crush her beneath
> their shields.
>
> *Herodias.* Nay, but it is infamous.
>
> *The Voice of Iokanaan.* It is thus that I will wipe out all
> wickedness from the earth, and that all women shall
> learn not to imitate her abominations. [*Salome*, p. 42]

Herodias mistakenly thinks the attack is leveled against her,
but she is flattering herself: it is Salome who is now the object
of Iokanaan's attack. The first thing Iokanaan had noticed
about Salome was her "golden eyes" and her "gilded eyelids,"
and he had called her a "daughter of Babylon." The repetition of these images strongly suggests that the daughter has
now displaced the mother in the prophet's mind. This is
reinforced when Herod points out to Herodias that Iokanaan
did not speak her name.

The verbal attack on Salome, like the earlier one on her
mother, is again suggestive of many meanings. The prophet's
cry for Salome's death reflects his murderous nature. A sword
is an explicit phallic symbol, moreover, and Iokanaan's desire
to see Salome pierced with swords—swords controlled and

directed by him—suggests his repressed lust for her. At the same time, he wants to see her destroyed and hidden from view by shields. The prophet's end—a severed head, eyes closed, in a position of sexual "intercourse" with Salome—sums up the essence and horror of Iokanaan. He possesses the object of his desire, but is, and will forever remain, unconscious of the fact.

Iokanaan dies physically, but Herod, his mirror opposite, dies spiritually: he becomes a Christian. Herod is an evil and lustful man who lives incestuously with the wicked Herodias. The night of the feast, however, his lust exceeds all bounds and he offers Salome the throne of her mother. At the same time, he fearfully reacts against the evil in himself. This is his reaction when Salome consents to dance for him:

> *Herod.* Pour water on my hands. Give me snow to eat. Loosen my mantle. Quick! quick! loosen my mantle. Nay, but leave it. It is my garland that hurts me, my garland of roses. The flowers are like fire. They have burned my forehead. (*He tears the wreath from his head, and throws it on the table.*) Ah! I can breathe now. How red those petals are! They are like stains of blood on the cloth. [*Salome*, p. 51]

His garland of roses becomes for him a crown of thorns. He tears it off his head at this stage, but only to put it on again at the end of the play. Herod recognizes Salome as the visible manifestation of his evil soul, and when she fully reveals her own nature, the vision proves too terrible for the Tetrarch to bear. The play ends thus:

> *Herodias.* I am well pleased with my daughter. She has done well. And I would stay here now.
> *Herod.* (*Rising.*) Ah! there speaks my brother's wife! Come! I will not stay in this place. Surely some terrible thing will befall. Manasseh, Issachar, Ozias, put out the torches. I will not look at things, I will not suffer things

to look at me. Put out the torches! Hide the moon!
Hide the stars! Let us hide ourselves in our palace,
Herodias. I begin to be afraid.

*(The slaves put out the torches. The stars disappear.
A great cloud crosses the moon and conceals it completely. The stage becomes quite dark. The Tetrarch
begins to climb the staircase.)*

The voice of Salome. Ah! I have kissed thy mouth,
Iokanaan, I have kissed thy mouth. There was a bitter
taste on thy lips. Was it the taste of blood? . . . Nay;
but perchance it was the taste of love. . . . They say
that love hath a bitter taste. . . . But what matter? I
have kissed thy mouth, Iokanaan, I have kissed thy
mouth.

*(A ray of moonlight falls on Salome and illumines
her.)*

Herod. (Turning round and seeing Salome.) Kill that
woman!

*(The soldiers rush forward and crush beneath their
shields Salome, daughter of Herodias, Princess of
Judæa.)* [*Salome,* pp. 66–67]

The cult of Cybele and Christianity stand opposed in
Salome. The former religion advocates the total, uninhibited
expression of human nature, which is evil—Cybele pierces the
darkness and illumines her Daughter [8] with an eerie moon-
beam—while the latter religion advocates the repression of
human nature. Herod, long a follower of Cybele, finally goes
too far, recoils, and becomes a Christian. His emphasis now is
on blindness, on the putting out of lights and the hiding of

8. For Wilde, the daughter of Herodias is the Daughter of Cybele, just
as the son of Mary—for Christianity—is also the Son of God. At one
point in the play, Herod accuses Herodias of being sterile, and when she
points to her daughter as proof of her fertility, Herod brushes the argument aside and reasserts that his wife is sterile. What Wilde is darkly suggesting is that Salome was born of a sterile mother because Cybele desired the birth to take place. Salome's conception, then, would be a kind
of evil Immaculate Conception.

things, especially of himself. The sight of Salome is no longer tolerable to him, and he orders her killed. The shields that crush her not only kill her but also hide her from the Tetrarch's view. The man who at the beginning of the play had maintained that "it is ridiculous to kill one's-self," at the end of the play does precisely that. Iokanaan had prophesied correctly when he foretold of Herod: "He shall be seated on his throne. He shall be clothed in scarlet and purple. In his hand he shall bear a golden cup full of his blasphemies. And the angel of the Lord shall smite him. He shall be eaten of worms" (*Salome*, p. 47). The death of Salome is the spiritual death of the Tetrarch.

Of the four main characters in *Salome*, only Herodias remains alive and unharmed. The "moral" of *Salome* is so subservient to the play's main theme as to be hardly noticeable, but there is a moral nonetheless. In *The Picture of Dorian Gray*, the moral was that all excess, as well as all renunciation, brings its punishment, and that a point of balance between the two must be found and maintained. The same is true of *Salome*. Iokanaan's total repression of his evil nature leads to his spiritual death, then to his physical death. Salome's total and uninhibited expression of her evil nature leads ultimately to her death. Herod's excesses trigger a reaction in him, and he finally recoils and fully represses his nature.

Herodias, on the other hand, maintains a point of balance between evil and renunciation. Her existence is a lustful and sin-scarred one, but she always exercises some restraint. Although it is true she lives incestuously with Herod, it was Herod who forcibly took her from his brother. Although she suggests to Herod that he hand Iokanaan over to the Jews, she does not insist. Although she fully approves of Salome's request for Iokanaan's head, she does not make the request herself. She fully enjoys Salome's terrible feast, but she does not participate in it. Consequently, she remains alive and well at the end of the play, while Salome, Iokanaan, and Herod are all punished for failing to maintain a point of balance.

In the end, it is Herodias who emerges as the norm of *Salome*. Herodias not only maintains a point of balance, moreover, but is herself a point of balance. To live in sin with Herodias, as Herod does, is still to be in balance, but to reach lustfully for a higher and more evil erotic relationship is to upset all balance and invite disaster. Of the three women in the play—Cybele, Salome, and Herodias—Herodias is the least evil, and it is unsafe in life to go beyond her.

In art, however, there is no need for this sort of balance, and one can build a shrine to Cybele and write a play whose main theme is the celebration and deification of Salome and her terrible, sinful lust. This is precisely what Wilde does in *Salome*. With Satanic glee, he slowly unmasks the true essence of human nature, until the play reaches its powerful climax and the mask is entirely ripped off. The ending is calculated to send a shock of horror through the audience, and Wilde leaves them in a state of shock. He himself is perfectly satisfied with the vision of human nature as evil, and does not—like Shakespeare in *King Lear,* for example—make any attempt to go beyond it.

The decadents wanted to force the Victorians to confront the evil within the human soul, and Wilde's play, correctly produced, is a tremendous success in this respect. The play absolutely reeks of evil, and any production of it that does not recognize this and convey a demonic atmosphere that steadily mounts toward an evil Apocalypse does not do justice to Wilde's genius.

Finally, it is important to note that Salome and Iokanaan represent two aspects of decadent art. They are both compared to art objects many times in the play. The decadents saw the human soul as evil and celebrated this evil. Salome is a symbol of the human soul, and she regards evil not only as a reality but as a feast. She fully represents one aspect of decadent art. Along with the celebration of evil, however, decadent art manifested a very pronounced death wish. The death wish is clear, for instance, in John Gray's "On a Picture," which lingers on the suicide of Ophelia, but is at its most apparent

in Lionel Johnson's "Nihilism," of which these are the final
two stanzas:

> Only the rest! the rest! only the gloom,
> Soft and long gloom! The pausing from all thought!
> My life, I cannot taste: the eternal tomb
> Brings me the peace, which life has never brought.
>
> For all the things I do, and do not well;
> All the forced drawings of a mortal breath:
> Are as the hollow music of a bell,
> That times the slow approach of perfect death.[9]

Decadent art also exhibited a Christian impulse that the
decadents, to a man, finally yielded to in their lives. In John
Gray's *Silverpoints,* the poem "A Crucifix" appears alongside
some of the most evil poetry written during the decade. Gray
writes in "A Crucifix," describing "Christ's unutterable
charm":

> "Behold the man!" Robust and frail. Beneath
> That breast indeed might throb the Sacred Heart.
> And from the lips, so holily despart,
> The dying murmur breathes "Forgive! Forgive!"
> O wide-stretched arms! "I perish, let them live."
> Under the torture of the thorny crown,
> The loving pallor of the brow looks down
> On human blindness, on the toiler's woes;
> The while, to overturn Despair's repose,
> And urge to Hope and Love, as Faith demands,
> Bleed, bleed the feet, the broken side, the hands.[10]

In "Carmelite Nuns of the Perpetual Adoration," [11] Ernest
Dowson combines the Christian impulse with the death wish.

9. Lionel Johnson, *Poetical Works of Lionel Johnson,* p. 243.
10. John Gray, *Silverpoints,* p. xxiii.
11. Ernest Dowson, "Carmelitus Nuns of the Perpetual Adoration." In
The Book of the Rhymers' Club (London: Elkin Mathews, 1892), pp. 10–
11. The poem sometimes appears under the briefer title, "Nuns of the

Dowson's attitude toward Catholicism is ambivalent in the poem. He praises the Catholic nuns who have rejected the world and achieved a "serene insight" into "the illuminating dawn" that will come after death, but he seems to be attracted to Catholicism mainly because it offers a deathlike state of calm. Indeed, his nuns seem as dead as Arnold's monks in "Stanzas From the Grande Chartreuse." He ends the poem by declaring that the world is noisy and passionate and wild, "But there, beside the altar, there, is rest."

Wilde, in *Salome,* fuses the Christian impulse with the death wish in the figure of Iokanaan, and presents both as forms of repression. Iokanaan is a Christian prophet, but he also lives in a tomblike cistern and voluntarily returns to it as an alternative to Salome. He regards death as an ally and repeatedly speaks of it as an angel. The coming of the angel of death does not disturb him in the least, while the beating of the angel's wings, by contrast, sends a chill through Herod. It is a deathlike quality in Iokanaan that attracts Salome, and his colors—white, black, and red—are the colors of death. Finally, when the executioner descends into the cistern to behead Iokanaan, the prophet makes no resistance at all. Death is welcome to Iokanaan, for it is a more adequate form of repression than Christianity. Iokanaan, then, is an embodiment and an interpretation of that aspect of decadent art which does not celebrate the evil within the self.

The highly artificial style of *Salome* is also characteristic of the decadents and, along with extreme symbolism, is a rebellion against the Victorian world's tendency to force a given style upon the artist and an assertion of the artist's superiority to his environment. At their best, however, the decadents used their artificial style functionally, and this is certainly the case with *Salome.* The rhythmic movement of the play's sentences, the subtle monotony of the repetitions, the haunting, sug-

Perpetual Adoration." This is the case in *The Poems of Ernest Dowson,* ed. Mark Longaker (Philadelphia: University of Pennsylvania Press, 1962), p. 43.

gestive symbolism, and the pronounced biblical flavor create a sense of the unearthly and the mysterious. As the play progresses, the style becomes a Black Mass that fuses perfectly with the religion of evil presented in *Salome*, reinforcing it while being reinforced by it.

In its closeness to music, moreover, the play's style shows the influence of Baudelaire's theory of "correspondances," advanced in *Les Fleurs du Mal*, which stressed the relationship between painting and music on the one hand and poetry on the other. In this respect, Wilde's prose-poem is again typically decadent, for—as John Munro has observed—"the Decadents in particular" were influenced by "Baudelaire's theory of 'les correspondances.' " [12] Wilde was probably also influenced by Pater's idea, expressed in his famous essay on Giorgione, that all art perpetually strives toward the condition of music, for in music alone is there a complete unity of form and content. The Beardsley illustrations further underline the interrelatedness of the arts, and are for that reason an integral part of *Salome*—a very successful attempt to capture graphically the essence of a play that constantly approaches pictorial definition. *Salome* strains at once toward the condition of music and of painting.

To end, it should be noted that *Salome* is probably meant to counterpoint *Endymion*. Never in his career did Oscar Wilde abandon the view that individual human beings begin in the world of innocence. The young Syrian's vision of Salome as angelic is a direct result of his youth. His angelic vision is entirely false, but only age, only the process of growing up, could have shattered it. Judging from Wilde's early poetry, Keats was his favorite author. The influence of Keats,

12. John M. Munro, introduction to *English Poetry in Transition, 1880–1920*, ed. John M. Munro (New York: Pegasus, 1968), p. 25. See also James Nelson's analysis of Arthur Symons's poem, "Javanese Dancers," in *The Early Nineties*, pp. 192–95. Nelson observes that "the poem is in its form an integral part of the impression being created," with the words and verse lines musically reflecting the strange, disquieting, harmonious movement of the dancers.

moveover, lies heavy upon the entire aesthetic-decadent movement. Keats died very young, though, and Shelley, in *Adonais*,
saw him as having escaped the contagion of the world's slow
stain through his early death.

Wilde did not escape this contagion, and *Salome* may be
seen as the demon universe's reply to *Endymion*. Like *Endymion*, it is a moon-dominated work, but its moon is in contrast to Keats's. Like *Endymion*, it is a heavily erotic work,
but its eroticism is sin-scarred, perverse, and hellish. In both
works, moreover, the eroticism has definite religious overtones.
There are three women in *Salome*, and they represent the
same principle in a descending order. They parallel the three
women of *Endymion*, who also represent one principle in a
descending order. Finally, Iokanaan contrasts with Endymion
in his reaction to the women of *Salome*. Endymion yearned to
burst his mortal bonds and unite with a divine essence.
Iokanaan, on the other hand, prefers physical and spiritual
imprisonment to union with such a terrible divinity as Cybele-
Salome.

The decadents were fond of playing off the Romantic vision
against their own vision of evil. John Gray does this quite
well in some of the poems of *Silverpoints*. In "Poem," for
instance—quoted in full in chapter 2 (p. 60—the "foul child"
is the opposite of the Romantic child and nature is presented
as evil and leprous, the antithesis of the Wordsworthian view
of nature. The metal statue of Robert Burns is entirely out of
place in Gray's evil garden. The Romantic poet remains silent
while the irreverent sparrows that flutter around him sing
in abandoned ecstasy.[13] If *Salome* is indeed meant as a

13. In "Mishka," Gray counterpoints Keats's "La Belle Dame Sans
Merci." The poet-bear Mishka is hypnotized by the beauty of an en-
chantress, an ominous monster-bee, and he follows her "into her lair/
Dragged in the net of her yellow hair." Mishka finds himself in an exotic
realm, a paradise, but unlike Keats's knight-at-arms, he never wakes on
the cold hill's side. Rather, he is maintained in a state of erotic, sensuous
joy, with "the honey-child's lips" forever glued to his mouth. In the embrace of a monster, evil and dripping with delicious honey, he finds

counterpoint to *Endymion,* then it stands as the decadents' most successful reply to a Romantic poet. If not, then it still exists as the one unquestionable masterpiece of the English decadence—the one work that binds together all the different threads of that literary tradition, interprets them, and presents them with overpowering excellence. The journal *Studio* was correct when it observed in 1894 that *Salome* is "the very essence of the decadent *fin de siècle*." [14]

Wilde was a man who was fascinated by paradox and found it to be his most efficient means of communication. *A Woman of No Importance* exists as a deliberate paradox; it offers a contrast to *Salome* in its comic atmosphere while essentially restating the play's main theme. In *Salome,* Wilde tried to bring the Victorians to a shocking and terrifying confrontation with the evil in human nature, but the play was banned from the English stage by the censors. In *A Woman of No Importance,* he tried again to identify human nature as evil, but this time he chose to take the road of comic subtlety. As Lord Illingworth observes: "To get into the best society, nowadays, one has either to feed people, amuse people, or shock people." [15] Wilde was not rich enough to feed people, and his attempt to shock them had been banned from the English stage because of a technicality regarding the use of biblical characters. Wilde must have strongly suspected, though, that it was the overt demonic atmosphere of *Salome* that had led to its censorship. Indeed, the London *Times* was typical of the general English reaction to *Salome* when it characterized the play as "an arrangement in blood and ferocity, morbid, *bizarre*, repulsive, and very offensive in its adaptation of scriptu-

eternal ecstasy and acquires the ultimate knowledge—a visionary knowledge of all things.
14. *Studio* 2 (Feb. 15, 1894): 184.
15. Oscar Wilde, *A Woman of No Importance,* ed. Robert Ross, p. 111. All future references to *A Woman of No Importance* are to this edition and are cited in parentheses in the text. The play will be designated as *Woman.*

ral phraseology to situations the reverse of sacred." [16] In *A Woman of No Importance,* Wilde attempted to elevate his social position by amusing people.

The main theme of *A Woman of No Importance* is that, despite apparent differences, human beings are basically alike —that is, totally corrupt. This theme is very cleverly camouflaged, though, and the play can be read simply as an amusing and rather touching work of art with no great originality or literary value. Wilde had written of *Salome:* "Ici et là, il y a des lacunes, mais l'idée du drame est claire" (*Letters,* p. 306). In *A Woman of No Importance,* on the other hand, the main idea is deliberately suppressed and befogged. The essential similarity among human beings is indicated in act 3:

> *Lady Hunstanton.* What did Sir John talk to you about, dear Mrs. Allonby?
>
> *Mrs. Allonby.* About Patagonia.
>
> *Lady Hunstanton.* Really? What a remote topic! But very improving, I have no doubt.
>
> *Mrs. Allonby.* He has been very interesting on the subject of Patagonia. Savages seem to have quite the same views as cultured people on almost all subjects. They are excessively advanced.
>
> *Lady Hunstanton.* What do they do?
>
> *Mrs. Allonby.* Apparently everything.
>
> *Lady Hunstanton.* Well it is very gratifying, dear Archdeacon, is it not, to find that Human Nature is permanently one.—On the whole, the world is the same world, is it not? [*Woman,* pp. 122–23]

The sexual practices of the Patagonian savages were far from what the Victorians would have considered proper. Mrs. Allonby—who, at this point, is carrying on a subtle flirtation with Sir John—says they do "apparently everything," and finds them very close to cultured people. Lady Hunstanton, without understanding her, is gratified "that Human Nature

16. Quoted in *Letters,* p. 335, n. 4.

is permanently one" and amusingly expresses her gratification to none other than the archdeacon. The main theme of *A Woman of No Importance* is that lust, in its hundred different manifestations, is the hallmark of human nature, the one thread that binds human beings together. The basic split in the play is between those characters who give free expression to their libidinous nature and those who mask it from others and from themselves. The aristocrats of the play wear no masks. This is made apparent in act 1, which is dominated by the conversation of a group of aristocrats on a garden lawn; but the wit is not harmless: it is, for the most part, an attack on the Victorian sexual code, or rather, a careless dismissal of it in favor of sexual looseness. This is clearly indicated later on:

> *Lady Hunstanton. (Shakes her fan at him.)* I don't know how it is, dear Lord Illingworth, but everything you have said to-day seems to me excesively immoral. It has been most interesting, listening to you. [*Woman,* p. 126]

The chief wits of the play are Lord Illingworth and Mrs. Allonby, and act 1 ends with a thinly veiled invitation from her to Illingworth to have an affair:

> *Lord Illingworth.* Shall we go in to tea?
> *Mrs. Allonby.* Do you like such simple pleasures?
> *Lord Illingworth.* I adore simple pleasures. They are the last refuge of the complex. But, if you wish, let us stay here. The Book of Life begins with a man and a woman in a garden.
> *Mrs. Allonby.* It ends with Revelations.
> *Lord Illingworth.* You fence divinely. But the button has come off your foil. [*Woman,* p. 44]

The curtain drops after two pass up the terrace, smiling at each other.

Much of the wit of *A Woman of No Importance* is borrowed from Lord Henry Wotton. This is Wilde at his laziest, but the borrowings do serve an important purpose. Lord Henry was corrupt, and the people who speak as he spoke identify themselves compactly as being corrupt. Wotton has been broken up into fragments, as it were, and now appears diffusely as the entire British aristocracy, though he is at his most concentrated in Lord Illingworth. The play is a comedy, but the shadow of Wotton casts its sinister length across it, suggesting dark, hidden meanings beneath the sparkling surface.

Opposed to the aristocrats in act 1 stands Mr. Kelvil, a member of the House of Commons, who is preparing a lecture on his favorite subject, purity. There is also the American girl, Hester Worsley, one of the chief characters in the play, whose attitude toward life is unyieldingly puritanical. Hester, however, has not yet come of age. Mrs. Allonby remarks: "She told me yesterday, and in quite a loud voice too, that she was only eighteen. It was most annoying" (Woman, p. 37). Hester is an innocent, and she is appropriately in love with another innocent, Gerald Arbuthnot. "Mr. Arbuthnot," she exclaims enthusiastically, "has a beautiful nature! He is so simple, so sincere. He has one of the most beautiful natures I have ever come across. It is a privilege to meet him" (Woman, pp. 4-5).

Mrs. Arbuthnot is only mentioned in act 1, but in act 2 we meet her: "MRS. ARBUTHNOT enters from terrace behind in a cloak with a lace veil over her head" (Woman, p. 72). She first appears as a cloaked and veiled woman, but the thrust of the play is to strip away the veils that obscure her corrupt nature. She is a church-going woman, deeply committed to the housing of the poor, and she is introduced to Hester in the following manner:

Lady Hunstanton. (to Miss Worsley) Now, do come, dear, and make friends with Mrs. Arbuthnot. She is one of the good, sweet, simple people you told us we never admitted into society. I am sorry to have to say Mrs. Arbuthnot comes very rarely to me. But that is not my fault. [Woman, p. 75]

As it turns out, however, Mrs. Arbuthnot once had an affair with Lord Illingworth when they were both very young, and Gerald is the illegitimate issue of that affair. The theme of the virtuous maiden seduced by the wicked aristocrat was a common one in Victorian literature, and Mrs. Arbuthnot sees herself as a poor, abandoned maiden who has had to lead a life of suffering because of Lord Illingworth's wickedness. Her view of her situation is not quite accurate, however:

> Lord Illingworth. You forget, Rachel, it was you who left me. It was not I who left you.
>
> Mrs. Arbuthnot. I left you because you refused to give the child a name. Before my son was born, I implored you to marry me.
>
> Lord Illingworth. I had no expectations then. And besides, I wasn't much older than you were. I was only twenty-two. I was twenty-one, I believe, when the whole thing began in your father's garden.

He continues: "As for saying I left our child to starve, that, of course, is untrue and silly. My mother offered you six hundred a year. But you wouldn't take anything. You simply disappeared, and carried the child with you" (*Woman*, pp. 92–93). Mrs. Arbuthnot's behavior is logically inexplicable, but sentiment has a logic of its own and it is tempting to explain her behavior sentimentally. This is not the case, however. Lord Illingworth observes: "You talk sentimentally, but you are thoroughly selfish the whole time" (*Woman*, p. 95). As the play unfolds, this view of Mrs. Arbuthnot is fully substantiated.

The garden imagery of *A Woman of No Importance* is a crucial key to the play's meaning. "The Book of Life begins with a man and a woman in a garden," Lord Illingworth observes in act 1, and Mrs. Allonby replies that "it ends with Revelations." Illingworth's affair with Mrs. Arbuthnot had begun in her father's garden, and in act 1 Mrs. Allonby begins a tentative affair with him in a garden. Gardens and flowers

are associated in the play with lust and sin. Mrs. Allonby, in
act 1, wishes to walk to the conservatory because "Lord
Illingworth told me this morning that there was an orchid
there as beautiful as the seven deadly sins" (*Woman,* p. 25).
Given these previous associations, it is disturbing when Mrs.
Arbuthnot uses garden imagery when referring to her son in
act 2:

> *Mrs. Arbuthnot.* George, don't take my son away from
> me. I have had twenty years of sorrow, and I have only
> had one thing to love me, only one thing to love. You
> have had a life of joy, and pleasure, and success. You
> have been quite happy, you have never thought of us.
> There was no reason, according to your views of life,
> why you should have remembered us at all. Your
> meeting us was a mere accident, a horrible accident.
> Forget it. Don't come now, and rob me of . . . of all
> I have in the whole world. You are so rich in other
> things. Leave me the little vineyard of my life; leave
> me the walled-in garden and the well of water; the ewe-
> lamb God sent me, in pity or in wrath, oh! leave me
> that. George, don't take Gerald from me. [*Woman,* p.
> 97]

Gerald is compared to a vineyard and a walled-in garden. A
faint fragrance of incest begins to fill the air, but the odor
remains very faint at this point.

In the clash over Gerald between Lord Illingworth and
Mrs. Arbuthnot in act 2, Illingworth emerges the victor, and
the act ends when he leads Gerald to the terrace. Act 3 begins
with a scene that is highly reminiscent of *The Picture of
Dorian Gray.* Illingworth is lecturing Gerald on life in very
much the same words that Wotton used to corrupt Dorian:

> *Gerald.* But I am so ignorant of the world, Lord Illing-
> worth.
> *Lord Illingworth.* Don't be afraid, Gerald. Remember
> that you've got on your side the most wonderful thing

in the world—youth! There is nothing like youth. The middle-aged are mortgaged to Life. The old are in life's lumber-room. But youth is the Lord of Life. Youth has a kingdom waiting for it. [*Woman,* p. 106]

Gerald responds positively to the lecture and takes Illingworth as his spiritual father: "Lord Illingworth is a successful man. He is a fashionable man. He is a man who lives in the world and for it. Well, I would give anything to be just like Lord Illingworth" (*Woman,* pp. 138–39). Gerald's true nature is rapidly emerging from the protective shell of innocence, as Dorian's had, and he shows a keen eagerness to embrace Lord Illingworth's dazzling, corrupt world. Mrs. Arbuthnot, in an effort to dissuade him, tells him the story of a very young maiden who was ruined by Illingworth; but Gerald places a heavy share of the blame on the young maiden, then lightly dismisses the matter, refusing to believe such stories about Lord Illingworth. Quite rightly, he is unwilling to risk his career because of Illingworth's possible past sexual adventures.

Gerald, however, is in love with Hester Worsley, and Illingworth has made a bet to convert Hester from Puritanism. As Gerald converses with his mother, Illingworth tries to kiss Hester in the garden. She reacts with puritanical terror, and Gerald leaps to her defense, swearing he will kill Lord Illingworth. To stop him, Mrs. Arbuthnot reveals that Illingworth is his father. Hester steals quietly off, Mrs. Arbuthnot faints, and the act ends with Gerald tenderly leading his mother away. Act 2 had ended with Gerald squarely in his father's camp, but act 3 ends with him moving back into that of mother. Indeed, the mother's revelation effectively isolates him in a separate world with her.

Act 4 is the most interesting act of the play, for in it Mrs. Arbuthnot shows herself—to the perceptive reader or viewer —as a true daughter of Herodias, a cultured Victorian version of Salome. In this act, she reveals the true reasons why she abandoned Illingworth as soon as their child was born. One reason is that the child displaced the father as the object of

her affection and she wanted him entirely for herself: she took
the male child for her lover and ran away with him. In a gush
of emotion, Mrs. Arbuthnot explains herself to Gerald:

> *Mrs. Arbuthnot.* No office is too mean, no care too lowly
> for the thing we women love—and oh! how *I* loved *you*.
> Not Hannah, Samuel more. And you needed love, for
> you were weakly, and only love could have kept you
> alive. Only love can keep any one alive. . . .
>   You thought I spent too much of my time in going
> to Church, and in Church duties. But where else could
> I turn? God's house is the only house where sinners are
> made welcome, and you were always in my heart,
> Gerald, too much in my heart. For, though day after
> day, at morn or evensong, I have knelt in God's house,
> I have never repented of my sin. How could I repent
> of my sin when you, my love, were its fruit! Even now
> that you are bitter to me I cannot repent. I do not.
> You are more to me than innocence. I would rather be
> your mother—oh! much rather!—than have always
> been pure. . . . Oh, don't you see? don't you under-
> stand? [*Woman,* pp. 166–69]

The fruit of Mrs. Arbuthnot's adventure in her father's
garden was Gerald, and she has been feasting on that fruit
ever since. The fragrance of incest is no longer faint but very
strong. Mrs. Arbuthnot's name—Rachel—also indicates her
incestuous character, for the biblical Rachel was both Jacob's
cousin and, along with her sister Leah, his wife. Jacob, moreover, was a younger brother who cheated his elder brother
Esau of the rights and privileges of seniority. Wilde is very
clever, though, for it is possible to see Mrs. Arbuthnot as a
sentimental, tender-hearted mother. The mask is lifted only
for the very perceptive. Mrs. Arbuthnot herself seems quite
blind to her incestuous feelings. She has placed upon her eyes,
not the covering of him who would see his God, but simply
the covering of excessive sentimentality.

Ironically, Hester overhears Mrs. Arbuthnot, rushes to her,

and embraces her. Hester had earlier declared that a man and a woman who have sinned should both be punished, but now she rejects her harsh Puritan attitude and insists that God's law is love. What she means, though, is that God's law is love for Gerald, since she shows no inclination whatsoever to forgive Lord Illingworth. The reason she forgives Mrs. Arbuthnot is because she recognizes a deep kinship with her: "In her all womanhood is martyred. Not she alone, but all of us are stricken in her house" (*Woman*, p. 170). Gerald had been insisting that his mother and Lord Illingworth marry, if only formally, for duty's sake.

Marriage, however, places the male in a dominant position, and what both Hester and Mrs. Arbuthnot seem to want is the opposite of this. In the parent-child relationship, the parent controls the child, and this is one reason Mrs. Arbuthnot had preferred Gerald to Illingworth. "You were weakly," she says to her son. Gerald, it seems, is destined to remain controlled. When he approaches Hester, she waves him back for having dared to insist that his mother marry Illingworth: "You cannot love me at all, unless you love her also. You cannot honour me, unless she's holier to you" (*Woman*, p. 170). The result is that Gerald withdraws his request, kneels before his mother, kisses her hands, and says: "You are my mother and my father all in one. I need no second parent" (*Woman*, p. 172).

It is only after Gerald has been literally brought to his knees that the two women are satisfied. Hester, moreover, has identified herself so thoroughly with Mrs. Arbuthnot that the latter now considers her an appropriate wife for Gerald:

> *Mrs. Arbuthnot. (Rises, and taking Hester by the hand, goes slowly over to where Gerald is lying on the sofa with his head buried in his hands. She touches him and he looks up.)* Gerald, I cannot give you a father, but I have brought you a wife.
>
> *Gerald.* Mother, I am not worthy either of her or you.
>
> *Mrs. Arbuthnot.* So she comes first, you are worthy. And when you are away, Gerald . . . with . . . her—oh,

think of me sometimes. Don't forget me. [*Woman*, p. 174]

Mrs. Arbuthnot had said earlier that she could not repent of her sin, and she does not repent now. She brings Gerald a girl in her own image and practically instructs the boy to think of his mother when he is making love to his wife. Vicariously, Mrs. Arbuthnot will remain Gerald's lover.

This incestuous marriage is given a final dramatic twist at the end of the play. Gerald and Hester are in the garden together, but the mother does not follow them, so they return to fetch her. Gerald kneels down beside his mother:

> *Mrs. Arbuthnot.* My boy! My boy! My boy! (*Running her fingers through his hair.*)
> *Hester.* (*Coming over.*) But you have two children now. You'll let me be your daughter?
> *Mrs. Arbuthnot.* (*Looking up.*) Would you choose me for a mother?
> *Hester.* You of all women I have ever known. [*Woman*, p. 190]

To the Victorians, this must have been a charming and tender scene. What has happened, though, is that Hester, by embracing Mrs. Arbuthnot as her mother, has symbolically made herself Gerald's sister. Her marriage to Gerald, then, is the marriage of a brother and sister.

It is a marriage, moreover, that will be dominated by Rachel Arbuthnot, who seems an inseparable part of it. Like the biblical Jacob, Gerald will have two wives, both incestuously related to him. Appropriately, the play ends with the three, intertwined like a spider web, withdrawing into the ubiquitous garden, the symbol of lust and sin. Mrs. Arbuthnot began her adult life in her father's garden with Lord Illingworth. Spiritually, she has never developed beyond that garden. Human nature being what it is, all human beings—Puritans included—enter the garden of Eros as soon as they emerge from the shell of innocence, and they remain there the rest of their lives.

Mrs. Arbuthnot is a woman of no importance because she is like everybody else in this respect.[17]

There is another reason, however, why Mrs. Arbuthnot abandoned Illingworth and ran away with Gerald. Cybele tore out Attis's sexual organs because he robbed her of her virginity. Salome killed Iokanaan to render him totally sterile. Mrs. Arbuthnot, being more civilized, robs Illingworth of his male child, the symbol of his virility. It is only years later, when Illingworth meets the grown Gerald and finds out who he is, that he fully discovers his need for the boy:

> Lord Illingworth. The world will know him merely as my private secretary, but to me he will be something very near, and very dear. It is a curious thing, Rachel; my life seemed to be quite complete. It was not so. It lacked something, it lacked a son. I have found by son now. I am glad I have found him. [Woman, p. 90]

To get Gerald back, he is ready to do anything, and he offers to marry Mrs. Arbuthnot and treat her always with deference and respect. She rejects the offer, however, and Lord Illingworth says: "Do tell me your reasons. They would interest me enormously." So she does:

> Mrs. Arbuthnot. We women live by our emotions and for them. By our passions and for them, if you will. I have two passions, Lord Illingworth: my love of him, my hate of you. You cannot kill those. They feed each other.
>
> Lord Illingworth. What sort of love is that which needs to have hate as its brother?

17. The purity-obsessed Mr. Kelvil gives vent to his lust within the framework of marriage and is the father of eight children. Lady Caroline, who invariably calls him Mr. Kettle, is not much mistaken, if we regard the kettle as a phallic symbol. Her mistake is double-edged, however, for it also reveals the reason for her interest in him—an interest that fades as soon as she discovers he is married and has a family. Even the archdeacon is a married man, though the state of his sexual impulse is indicated by the lamentable and deteriorating physical condition of his wife.

Mrs. Arbuthnot. It is the sort of love I have for Gerald.
Do you think that terrible? Well, it is terrible. All love
is terrible. [*Woman*, p. 185]

This is a clear echo of *Salome.* Mrs. Arbuthnot, by her own
admission, lives for passion, but what she seems to want is a
sterile affair of passion that protects her virginity. Her relationship with Gerald, and the continuation of it through
Hester, is for her the perfect love affair, for it constitutes no
threat whatsoever to her virginity. Such love, however, is of
necessity accompanied by a deep hatred of virile masculinity,
and Mrs. Arbuthnot savagely refuses to give Illingworth back
the symbol of his virility or to allow him any contact with it.
It is no accident that Illingworth is a bachelor and that he has
been unable, since his affair with Mrs. Arbuthnot, to have a
satisfying sexual relationship: "Upon my word, Rachel, no
woman ever loved me as you did. Why, you gave yourself to
me like a flower, to do anything I liked with" (*Woman*, pp.
188–89). His two sexual attempts in the play result in failure.
His affair with Mrs. Allonby never proceeds beyond the stage
of witty conversation, and he is violently repulsed by Hester.

The meeting ends with Lord Illingworth's attempt to hu-
miliate Mrs. Arbuthnot by relegating her to an inferior social
and sexual position, as he had done many years before. That
his attempt is meant as a replay of their original encounter
is indicated when Illingworth says: "How curious! At this
moment you look exactly as you looked the night you left me
twenty years ago. You have just the same expression in your
mouth" (*Woman*, p. 188). Mrs. Arbuthnot's response to Illingworth is quick, physical, and successful: she strikes him across
the face with his own glove, a phallic symbol. Stunned and
silent, he withdraws, a defeated man.

Finally, it should be pointed out that *A Woman of No
Importance* is probably meant as a response to Hawthorne's
The Scarlet Letter. Hawthorne was fascinated by his Puritan
ancestors and was the principal spokesman for a diluted Puritan ethic in nineteenth-century American literature. Wilde's

Hester is really out of the pages of *The Scarlet Letter,* as the
following exchange concerning her origin suggests. The conversation is largely out of *Dorian Gray,* but it is functional:

> *Lady Caroline.* Who are Miss Worsley's parents?
> *Lord Illingworth.* American women are wonderfully
> clever in concealing their parents.
> *Lady Hunstanton.* My dear Lord Illingworth, what do
> you mean? Miss Worsley, Caroline, is an orphan. Her
> father was a very wealthy millionaire or philanthropist,
> or both, I believe, who entertained my son quite hos-
> pitably, when he visited Boston. I don't know how he
> made his money, originally.
> *Kelvil.* I fancy in American dry goods.
> *Lady Hunstanton.* What are American dry goods?
> *Lord Illingworth.* American novels. [*Woman,* pp. 18–19]

In Hester Worsley are embodied the rigid beliefs and attitudes
of the Boston Puritan community of *The Scarlet Letter,* and
her father is really Nathaniel Hawthorne himself, a Boston
worthy who made his money writing "dry" novels. She is
hilariously undercut throughout the play, and she ends up by
identifying herself with Mrs. Arbuthnot. Mrs. Arbuthnot, a
sinful woman left with only her child, suggests Hester Prynne
and little Pearl. Just as Hester fought to keep Pearl, so Mrs.
Arbuthnot fights to keep Gerald, even using Hester's argument
that God gave the child to her. Whereas Hester Prynne
achieves genuine penitence at the end of the novel, however,
Mrs. Arbuthnot never repents. Pearl—suspected of being a
demon offspring and an elf-child—ultimately proves to be, at
least partially, the God-sent instrument of her parents' salvation; but Gerald is truly a demon offspring. He is Satan's gift
to Mrs. Arbuthnot, as it were, and through him she manages
to perpetuate her sin.

Roger Chillingworth appears in Hawthorne's novel as a
physically deformed, sexually impotent man with a powerful
intellect, who has committed an intellectual sin. Similarly,
George Illingworth is impotent and physically misshapen, but

this because Mrs. Arbuthnot has symbolically torn out his sexual organs. The symbol of his shame is not a scarlet letter but the absence of two letters from his surname—the *ch* of Chillingworth. This idea is reinforced if we recognize that the names Roger and George are composed of precisely the same letters. Illingworth's predicament reduces him to a point where he can only sin intellectually, and he does have a tremendous intellect that he uses sinfully, to invent corrupt epigrams and immoral wit.

Reverend Dimmesdale is also not forgotten by Wilde in *A Woman of No Importance*. Without exaggeration, he is the play itself. Outwardly a holy and respected man, Dimmesdale was in reality a sinner who hid his crime from the world. His entire existence was a lie. This is also true of Wilde's play. Outwardly conventional and respectable, it conceals within itself a terrible, sinful truth about human nature. Whereas Dimmesdale was convulsed and tortured by his secret sin, Wilde is placid and serene about the dark truth hidden away in his comedy. Dimmesdale moved toward an agonized revelation of his sin, and saved his soul as a consequence. Wilde's play does not move toward such a revelation, nor does it hint at all that human nature is capable of goodness. As in *Salome*, Wilde is here perfectly satisfied with his vision of human nature as evil and does not attempt in any way to transcend it.

A Woman of No Importance is a unique play; it is the only comedy the decadent movement ever produced. The funniest joke of the play, however, is one that only Oscar Wilde and his closest friends must have enjoyed at the time: Wilde had given the Victorians *Salome* once again, this time in the guise of a comedy with a large sentimental streak. The Victorians, failing to penetrate the façade and recognize the play's demonic content, applauded, and Wilde found himself a famous playwright. And not unjustly so. The play is a good and a challenging one, with definite Freudian overtones. A stage production that brings out its demonic content—perhaps by providing it with a heavily suggestive garden setting—may prove very interesting indeed.

4 Reaction

> Oh, that's nonsense, Algy. You never talk anything
> but nonsense.
>
> WILDE, *The Importance of Being Earnest*

So far, the development of Oscar Wilde has been toward a
steadily deepening exploration of the demon universe. *An
Ideal Husband,* however, evinces a return to the pattern of
the fairy tales. The play celebrates the power of love to
triumph over the fallen world and attain a state of higher
innocence. Neither Sir Robert Chiltern nor Lord Goring,
but Lady Chiltern is the central character in this play; the
action of the drama is based on her development from innocence to experience to a higher innocence.

The play begins with a reception at Sir Robert's house.
The opening scene is dominated by Lady Chiltern, who
stands at the top of a staircase receiving the guests as they
come up. There is something disturbingly artificial about the
reception, however: it hauntingly suggests a nonhuman art
world. Each of the guests, as he or she enters, is associated
with an artist or a work of art, for example: *"Enter* LORD
CAVERSHAM, *an old gentleman of seventy, wearing the riband
and star of the Garter. A fine Whig type. Rather like a
portrait by Lawrence."* [1] There are also references to exquisite pieces of furniture or tapestry, there is a music room
from which floats the sound of a string quartet, and the entire
house, with its great chandeliers and magnificent staircases,
suggests a work of art.

In this world Lady Chiltern is perfectly at home, but her

1. Oscar Wilde, *An Ideal Husband,* ed. Robert Ross, p. 4. All future
references to *An Ideal Husband* are to this edition and are cited in parentheses in the text. The play will be designated as *Husband.*

husband is not. When Sir Robert first appears—"*Vandyck would have liked to have painted his head*"—he is described as being nervous and self-conscious. He has every right to be nervous, for his wife sees him as inhumanly flawless and consequently he has to wear a permanent mask or lose her love. At one point, she refers to him as an ideal and a tower of ivory. At another point, she says: "You were to me something apart from common life, a thing pure, noble, honest, without stain. The world seemed to me finer because you were in it, and goodness more real because you lived" (*Husband*, p. 131). To Lady Chiltern, Sir Robert is "a thing," not a human being. These associations suggest an idol on a pedestal, a beautiful work of art, perfect and white and made of ivory.

Sir Robert, however, is not a work of art but a human being. Years before, at twenty-two, he had come of age and confronted the demon universe in the form of the Satanic Baron Arnheim, a wizard of modern European finance:

> *Sir Robert Chiltern.* One night after dinner at Lord Radley's the Baron began talking about success in modern life as something that one could reduce to an absolutely definite science. With that wonderfully fascinating quiet voice of his he expounded to us the most terrible of all philosophies, the philosophy of power, preached to us the most marvellous of all gospels, the gospel of gold. . . . I remember so well how, with a strange smile on his pale, curved lips, he led me through his wonderful picture gallery, showed me his tapestries, his enamels, his jewels, his carved ivories, made me wonder at the strange loveliness of the luxury in which he lived; and then told me that luxury was nothing but a background, a painted scene in a play, and that power, power over other men, power over the world, was the one thing worth having, the one supreme pleasure worth knowing, the one joy one never tired of, and that in our century only the rich possessed it. [*Husband*, pp. 80–81]

Sir Robert sells a state secret to the baron and thus acquires a fortune. He uses the money to go into the House immediately. "The Baron advised me in finance from time to time. Since then everything that I have touched has turned out a success" (*Husband,* pp. 84–85).

There is, in *An Ideal Husband,* a split between public life and private life. The public world is largely one of sordid speculations and self-seeking, power-hungry creatures, while the private world is beautiful, unsoiled, innocent. Lady Chiltern admits public life into her private world, but she sees it masked without realizing what is behind the mask. Sir Robert, though, is remarkably unsoiled for a public man. Despite his imperfections, he represents what is best in English public life and uses his wealth and power for good, never for evil. His sin belongs to the past, and it is important to note that the popular assessment of his career is correct. Far from being a villain, he is the purest sort of politician, waging constant war against fraudulence and injustice in the public domain. It is true that, to gain a position of power in the public domain, he had to resort to fraudulence, but such are the ironies of life and the necessities of the public world.

As for Lady Chiltern, she is less perfect than she imagines. Some of Wilde's fairy tales indicate that the world of innocence is not human. The happy prince, dying as an innocent, becomes a statue but is humanized in the course of the tale. In "The Fisherman and His Soul," the world of innocence is clearly not human. The same is true of Lady Chiltern's world of innocence; it is a place in which human beings, as though touched by a magic wand, become art objects upon entry. The imagery associated with Lady Chiltern, too, suggests a nonhuman quality. This is how act 2 ends: *"Pale with anguish, bewildered, helpless, she sways like a plant in the water. Her hands, outstretched, seem to tremble in the air like blossoms in the wind. Then she flings herself down beside a sofa and buries her face. Her sobs are like the sobs of a child"* (*Husband,* p. 133). Lady Chiltern is like a plant or a blossom, but plants and blossoms, though beautiful, are not human.

They represent a delightful but undeveloped form of life. There are higher forms, and Lady Chiltern, still a child, must move beyond her world if she is to attain a better and more noble existence.

The road, as in the fairy tales, is love. In her infant's world, Lady Chiltern "stands apart as good women do—pitiless in her perfection—cold and stern and without mercy" (*Husband*, p. 162). Her world of innocence, however, is destroyed by Baron Arnheim's mistress, Mrs. Cheveley, who rips the painted mask from Sir Robert's face and reveals the man beneath. Mrs. Cheveley is associated by Wilde with a lamia. When she enters Lord Goring's home in act 3, Wilde tells us that, "*Lamia-like, she is in green and silver*" (*Husband*, p. 150). She is a beautiful woman, but when Lord Goring snares her in a trap, she becomes hideous, both in her language—now punctuated by curses—and in her appearance: "*Her face is distorted. Her mouth awry. A mask has fallen from her. She is, for the moment, dreadful to look at*" (*Husband*, p. 101). A snake-bracelet fastened securely to her wrist causes the reaction. At any rate, Lady Chiltern faces this creature from the demon universe and finds that she must either develop beyond her or be destroyed by her. The road to salvation is clear. Lord Goring says to Lady Chiltern:

> *Lord Goring.* All I know is that life cannot be understood without much charity, cannot be lived without much charity. It is love, and not German philosophy, that is the true explanation of this world, whatever may be the explanation of the next. [*Husband*, p. 101]

Lady Chiltern lacks a developed heart, and it is this she must acquire if she is to save herself and her husband. Lord Goring saves Sir Robert from Mrs. Cheveley, but only Lady Chiltern's ability to move toward a higher innocence can really open up a new world for him:

> *Sir Robert Chiltern.* The sin of my youth, that I thought was buried, rose up in front of me, hideous, horrible,

with its hands at my throat. I could have killed it for
ever, sent it back into its tomb, destroyed its record,
burned the one witness against me. You prevented me.
No one but you, you know it. And now what is there
before me but public disgrace, ruin, terrible shame, a
lonely dishonoured life, a lonely dishonoured death, it
may be, some day? Let women make no more ideals
of men! let them not put them on altars and bow before
them, or they may ruin other lives as completely as you
—you whom I have so wildly loved—have ruined
mine! [*Husband*, pp. 132–33]

Lady Chiltern proves her husband wrong, however. In act
4, she does attain a higher innocence. She begins by forgiving
Sir Robert but encouraging him to withdraw from public
life. When Lord Caversham brings him the news that he has
been offered a seat in the Cabinet, Sir Robert is on the brink
of accepting *"when he sees his wife looking at him with her
clear, candid eyes. He then realises that it is impossible"* (*Husband*, p. 223). Lady Chiltern forgives her husband only within
the realm of private life, but Lord Goring intervenes:

Lord Goring. Lady Chiltern, allow me. You wrote me a
letter last night in which you said you trusted me and
needed my help. Now is the moment when you really
want my help, now is the time when you have got to
trust me, to trust in my counsel and judgment. You love
Robert. Do you want to kill his love for you? What
sort of existence will he have if you rob him of the
fruits of his ambition, if you take him from the splendour of a great political career, if you close the doors
of public life against him, if you condemn him to
sterile failure, he who was made for triumph and
success? Women are not meant to judge us, but to
forgive us when we need forgiveness. Pardon, not
punishment, is their mission. Why should you scourge
him with rods for a sin done in his youth, before he
knew you, before he knew himself? [*Husband*, p. 228]

As a result of Lord Goring's appeal, Lady Chiltern moves
toward total love of her husband. Having forgiven him in
private life, she now forgives him within the realm of public
life and tears up his negative letter to the Prime Minister.
In Wilde's later fairy tales, the higher innocence involved
a fusion of all opposites within a framework of love and
absolute purity, and this is precisely what Lady Chiltern
achieves at this stage. The public and the private are united
in love by her. Only when Lady Chiltern forgives him as a
public man is Sir Robert liberated from the power of Baron
Arnheim. Earlier, he had wished that the sin of his youth
could be burnt to ashes, and the wish comes true, but not only
when Lord Goring wrests the incriminating letter from Mrs.
Cheveley and burns it. The burning of the letter is necessary,
but the decisive step is when Lady Chiltern forgives her
husband as a public man. Both husband and wife, having faced
the demon universe and triumphed over it, leave its dregs
behind them. Never again will Sir Robert find himself a
prisoner of the past because of his wife's undeveloped nature.
From now on, he will be totally unhampered in his efforts
to purify the public domain. The play ends with the pair
entering a state of higher innocence:

> Sir Robert Chiltern. (*Taking her hand.*) Gertrude, is it
> love you feel for me, or is it pity merely?
> Lady Chiltern. (*Kisses him.*) It is love, Robert. Love, and
> only love. For both of us a new life is beginning. [*Husband,* p. 239]

Finally, it should be noted that Lord Goring's character
does not need to develop in the play because he already has,
when we first meet him, a heart overflowing with unselfish
love. His brush with the demon universe came many years
earlier, when he was briefly engaged to Mrs. Cheveley herself.
He hides his heart behind a trivial buttonhole and a non-
serious pose, but it shows nevertheless. His father continually
accuses him of being shallow but, ironically, it is the father
who is shallow, for he fails to recognize the reality behind the

delightful toy mask his son wears. It is to Mabel's credit that she is in love with Lord Goring.

An Ideal Husband is unquestionably a social comedy marred by a touch of mysogyny [2] and a too-heavy dependence on the devices of the well-made play. In its theme, however, it belongs with the fairy tales. Artistically, Wilde has veered sharply away from the sinister depths of *Salome*. The chill atmosphere of evil has been replaced by an atmosphere of love and forgiveness. *An Ideal Husband* opens with a description of the octagonal room at Sir Robert Chiltern's house, where *"over the well of the staircase hangs a great chandelier with wax lights, which illumine a large eighteenth-century French tapestry—representing the Triumph of Love, from a design by Boucher—that is stretched on the staircase wall"* (*Husband*, p. 1). And indeed, the triumph of love is what *An Ideal Husband* is basically about—although, paradoxically, love can triumph only after the art world of Boucher and great chandeliers and French tapestries has been transcended.

In *The Importance of Being Earnest*, Wilde's reaction against the demon universe takes a different form, and one more uniquely his own. The two most prominent words in the play are *nonsense* and *serious*, or their synonyms. This is entirely appropriate, since the play itself is a reduction of all seriousness to the level of nonsense. In it, Wilde pauses for a

2. "A man's life is of more value than a woman's" (*Husband*, p. 228), Lord Goring asserts, and both Sir Robert and Lady Chiltern readily concur in this view. *An Ideal Husband* is of interest biographically because what prevents Sir Robert from attaining a higher innocence for so long is his wife's innocent, undeveloped nature. The demon universe maintains its hold on Sir Robert because his wife refuses to acknowledge that *everyone* must come in contact with that universe at some time in his life, and consequently forces Sir Robert to hide the truth from her. Lady Chiltern's development probably reflects Wilde's wish that his wife Constance would develop in the same direction, thereby freeing him from the world of homosexual contacts. The mysogyny would then, perhaps, reflect his irritation with Constance for remaining innocent and unaware of the dark side of life.

space, takes a hard look at his career to date, and has a good, long laugh at himself. The play is absolutely devoid of sober content, and any attempt to find serious meaning in it must of necessity fall wide of the mark.

To say that the play has no serious meaning, however, is not to say that it has no meaning at all. Its very message, paradoxically, lies in its lack of seriousness, for here Oscar Wilde has a hearty laugh at his own expense. The target of the fun is Wilde's work up to this time. "Lord Arthur Savile's Crime," *The Picture of Dorian Gray, Salome, A Woman of No Importance,* even *An Ideal Husband*—Wilde singles out these works and, one by one, destroys their intellectual content, reducing them to the level of harmlessness and absurdity. Quite earnestly, he informs us that every serious thought he has had to date is nonsense—and very laughable nonsense at that.

The Importance of Being Earnest is essentially a private joke, though the source of its great popularity is Wilde's ability to translate the joke into public terms. By achieving and maintaining a perfect balance between the public and the private, Wilde managed to write one of the most brilliant comic masterpieces of the nineteenth century.

Oscar Wilde's works are often based on earlier ones. *The Picture of Dorian Gray* carefully counterpoints "Lord Arthur Savile's Crime" while providing *Lady Windermere's Fan* with its basic theme. *A Woman of No Importance* is thematically a repetition of *Salome,* while its wit is borrowed largely from *Dorian Gray. An Ideal Husband* harks back to the fairy tales in theme. *The Importance of Being Earnest* is the least self-contained of Wilde's works, for it is rooted not in one but in practically all of them. It is, moreover, an entirely original play. Wilde was later to write, in *De Profundis:* "I took the drama, the most objective form known to art, and I made it as personal a mode of expression as the lyric or the sonnet, at the same time that I widened its range and enriched its characterization" (*Letters,* p. 466).

If *Earnest* has exasperated the critics, it is because of this complete originality. Without doubt, it widened the range of the drama. Drama had been used subjectively before, by the Romantics, but Wilde here carried it to the outer limits of subjectivity and thus provided us with probably the most personal, private play in existence—a play that is basically a self-parody. Forever a lover of paradox, he took the most objective form known to literature and treated it entirely subjectively. The opening lines suggest what sort of a drama this is going to be:

> *Algernon.* Did you hear what I was playing, Lane?
>
> *Lane.* I didn't think it polite to listen, sir.
>
> *Algernon.* I'm sorry for that, for your sake. I don't play accurately—any one can play accurately—but I play with wonderful expression. As far as the piano is concerned, sentiment is my forte.[3]

Algy's piano-playing is an art, but he aims through it purely to express a mood. Lane regards this art as private and discreetly turns a deaf ear, but had he listened he would have had an enjoyable experience.

Like Algy's piano-playing, *The Importance of Being Earnest* aims purely at creating a mood, and it succeeds so brilliantly that audiences have been applauding since 1895. It is the object of this analysis to show that the play also has a private meaning that is wholly consistent with its humorous trivial mood. The meaning—not necessary to an enjoyment of *Earnest*—reinforces the mood and adds an extra comic dimension to the play. To see the play's dialogue as constituting an anti-Victorian barrage—as Eric Bentley does [4]—or to condemn it as depraved—as Mary McCarthy does [5]—is really to be

3. Oscar Wilde, *The Importance of Being Earnest*, ed. Robert Ross, p. 1. All future references to the three-act version of *The Importance of Being Earnest* are to this edition and are cited in parentheses in the text. The play will be designated as *Earnest*.

4. Eric Bentley, *The Playwright as Thinker*, pp. 172–77.

5. Mary McCarthy, *Mary McCarthy's Theatre Chronicles* (New York: Farrar, Strauss and Co., 1963), pp. 106–10.

untrue to its tone and unappreciative of its originality. Even Richard Ellmann misses the mark—though not by much—when he sees the play's theme as being sin and crime, treated indifferently and rendered harmless.[6]

Wilde parodies his earlier works haphazardly in *Earnest*, but in examining the play it is more organized to discuss these works in order of their composition. In "Lord Arthur Savile's Crime," Sybil was the erotic personification of all perfection, and Arthur had to undergo a symbolic baptism and murder the evil within himself in order to marry her. Gwendolyn and Cecily exist in this play partly—even entirely—as parodies of Sybil. Both dismiss any attempt on the part of their suitors to consider them perfect. For example:

> *Jack.* You're quite perfect, Miss Fairfax.
> *Gwendolyn.* Oh! I hope I am not that. It would leave no room for developments, and I intend to develop in many directions. [*Earnest*, p. 25]

Algy has a similar experience with Cecily:

> *Algernon.* I hope, Cecily, I shall not offend you if I state quite frankly and openly that you seem to me to be in every way the visible personification of absolute perfection.
> *Cecily.* I think your frankness does you great credit, Ernest. If you will allow me, I will copy your remarks into my diary. [*Earnest*, pp. 103–04]

Cecily comically undercuts the notion of her perfection by vainly dashing off to copy Algy's remarks into her diary. Her vanity is elaborated at some length in the original, four-act version of the play, which Wilde trimmed down for the stage at the insistence of George Alexander.[7]

6. Richard Ellmann, "Introduction: The Artist as Critic as Wilde," pp. xxvii–iii.

7. All references to the four-act version of *The Importance of Being Earnest* are to the play as it appears in *The Complete Works of Oscar Wilde*, ed. J. B. Foreman (London and Glasgow: Collins, 1970), pp. 321–

Indeed, any idea we may have had about the perfection of Cecily and Gwendolyn is dispelled by their verbal duel in act 2. Furthermore, they both end up with wicked husbands. Sybil—or Lady Chiltern, for that matter—would have died as a result, but Cecily and Gwendolyn remain quite happy and unharmed at the end of the play. Vice is a delightful, harmless thing in *Earnest:* it cannot destroy. Besides, a touch of wickedness in a man makes him all the more attractive, and Cecily's interest in Algy had begun when she heard how bad he was.

Arthur had to kill Podgers before he could marry Sybil, and both Jack and Algy find themselves forced to "commit murder" before they can marry the women they love. Jack says: "If Gwendolyn accepts me, I am going to kill my brother, indeed I think I'll kill him in any case" (*Earnest,* p. 21). Similarly, Algy "kills" Bunbury. In both cases, the person "killed" exists only in the imagination of the murderer, whereas Podgers existed both within and outside of Arthur. In neither case, moreover, does the "murder" lead to the purification of its perpetrator. Arthur's crime, hilarious to begin with, is here rendered entirely harmless and dissolves into complete nonsense.

Like Lord Arthur, Jack and Algy seem to have to undergo

84. In my analysis of *Earnest,* I have used the three-act version because I feel that Wilde, in trimming down the play and making it more compact, improved it in many ways. One major example is that he made Dr. Chasuble and Miss Prism more attractive comic figures by cutting many of their tedious, heavily moral lines. On the other hand, one can only regret that the delightful scene in which Algy is almost arrested was omitted in its entirety. On balance, though, the three-act *Earnest* must, I think, be considered superior.

Richard Ellmann seems to agree with this opinion, for in his *Selected Writings of Oscar Wilde* (London: Oxford University Press, 1961), he gives us the three-act version. When *The Importance of Being Earnest* was first published in February, 1899, moreover, Wilde issued the play in its revised, three-act version. Nevertheless, the four-act version is the fullest and most complete one, and it should definitely be referred to in any analysis of *Earnest.* In using the three-act version but constantly referring to the four-act one, I am following Richard Ellmann's example in his brief analysis of the play in "The Artist as Critic as Wilde."

a baptism of sorts before marriage can become possible. Unlike Arthur's bathtub baptism and its subsequent torments, however, theirs does not involve a spiritual rebirth but simply a change of name. Their baptism is a reductio ad absurdum of Arthur's. Arthur's agony of rebirth is mocked in the following passage:

> *Jack and Algernon.* We are going to be christened this afternoon.
> *Gwendolyn. (To Jack.)* For my sake you are prepared to do this terrible thing?
> *Jack.* I am.
> *Cecily. (To Algernon.)* To please me you are ready to face this fearful ordeal?
> *Algernon.* I am!
> *Gwendolyn.* How absurd to talk of the equality of the sexes! Where questions of self-sacrifice are concerned, men are infinitely beyond us. [*Earnest,* p. 152]

Nor does baptism turn out to be necessary in the end. It is discovered that Jack *is* Ernest, after all, and that Algy *is* his younger brother, known to Cecily as Ernest. Both escape the agony of a sprinkling by Chasuble.

In *Earnest, The Soul of Man Under Socialism* is cut to pieces in a few brief lines. In the essay, Wilde had advocated the abolition of private property and had tried to win over the rich by writing: "Property not only has duties, but has so many duties that its possession to any large extent is a bore. It involves endless claims upon one, endless attention to business, endless bother. If property had simply pleasures we could stand it; but its duties make it unbearable. In the interest of the rich we must get rid of it" (*Intentions,* p. 278). In *The Importance of Being Earnest,* the wealthy Lady Bracknell agrees with Wilde but finds a nonsocialistic solution to the problem:

> *Lady Bracknell.* What is your income?
> *Jack.* Between seven and eight thousand a year.

> *Lady Bracknell.* (*Makes a note in her book.*) In land, or in investments?
>
> *Jack.* In investments, chiefly.
>
> *Lady Bracknell.* That is satisfactory. What between the duties expected of one during one's lifetime, and the duties exacted from one after one's death, land has ceased to be either a profit or a pleasure. It gives one position, and prevents one from keeping it up. That's all that can be said about land. [*Earnest,* p. 42]

If private property is a bother, then by all means eliminate it—invest the money! As for the lower classes, whose poverty Wilde had seen in the essay as poisoning the lives of the rich, they are summarily dismissed at the beginning of the play when Algy says: "Lane's views on marriage seem somewhat lax. Really, if the lower classes don't set us a good example, what on earth is the use of them? They seem, as a class, to have absolutely no sense of moral responsibility" (*Earnest,* p. 4). Nor does Lady Bracknell seem at all upset about the existence of the lower classes. After all, they are not on her list of socially acceptable people—the same list as the duchess of Bolton's, no less! If Jack cannot produce socially acceptable parents, he cannot marry Gwendolyn, and that is the end of that.

The idea of determinism is prominent in both "Lord Arthur Savile's Crime" and *The Picture of Dorian Gray.* In *Salome,* too, Iokanaan, without understanding, correctly prophesies an evil Apocalypse. In *The Importance of Being Earnest,* Wilde has a good laugh at the expense of this concept. When Algy proposes to Cecily, he finds that he has already been engaged to her for three whole months and that the courting has already taken place. His future, he discovers, did not wait for him to bring it about but occurred without him:

> *Cecily.* I accepted you under this dear old tree here. The next day I bought this little ring in your name, and

this is the little bangle with the true lovers' knot I
promised you always to wear.

Algernon. Did I give you this? It's very pretty, isn't it?

Cecily. Yes, you've wonderfully good taste, Ernest. It's
the excuse I've always given for your leading such a
bad life. And this is the box in which I keep all your
dear letters. (*Kneels at table, opens box, and produces
letters tied up with blue ribbon.*)

Algernon. My letters! But, my own sweet Cecily, I have
never written you any letters.

Cecily. You need hardly remind me of that, Ernest. I
remember only too well that I was forced to write your
letters for you. I wrote always three times a week, and
sometimes oftener. [*Earnest,* pp. 107–08]

This goes on and on, as the concept of determinism is reduced to hilarious nonsense. And there is another comic jab at
predestination in the play. A prediction is made in act 1 that
fully materializes in act 2:

Jack. Cecily and Gwendolyn are perfectly certain to be
extremely great friends. I'll bet you anything you like
that half an hour after they have met, they will be calling each other sister.

Algernon. Women only do that after they have called
each other a lot of other things first. [*Earnest,* p. 55]

Cecily and Gwendolyn meet in act 2, and they do call each
other all sorts of terrible names for about half an hour, then
end up by calling each other—sister!

The Picture of Dorian Gray is also heavily parodied in *The
Importance of Being Earnest.* Dorian led a double life. The
picture of his soul was locked safely away in a dark room
while the innocent face he presented to respectable society was
only a mask. As society began to suspect the real Dorian, he
found himself shunned and avoided. His total unmasking—a
horror he is spared during his lifetime—would have meant
his irrevocable social ruin. Jack and Algy also lead double

lives. As with Dorian, their real self is the wicked one. Jack
explains to Algy that he wears a mask in the country for the
sake of his ward, Cecily: "When one is placed in the position
of guardian, one has to adopt a very high moral tone on all
subjects. It's one's duty to do so" (*Earnest*, p. 18).

Algy, on the other hand, assumes his façade in the city,
where he is constantly under the gaze of Lady Bracknell and
other respectable personages. The mask drops only when he
goes Bunburying. As the play moves to its climax, the respectable identities of Jack and Algy are discovered by all to be
fictional. Jack is found out—he is Ernest. Algy is also found
out—he is Jack's wicked younger brother Ernest. For both
Ernests, however, the result of this revelation is not ostracism
but marriage. By reducing Dorian's situation to the level of
farce and turning the unmasking into a happy event, Wilde
dismisses the protagonist of his novel with a roar of carefree
laughter.

The idea that paradoxes and epigrams have the power to
corrupt—prominent in *Dorian Gray*—is also ridiculed here.
Much of the wit of *The Importance of Being Earnest* is
sparkling, hilarious nonsense, as for instance:

> *Jack.* Everybody is clever nowadays. You can't go any-
> where without meeting clever people. The thing has
> become an absolute public nuisance. I wish to good-
> ness we had a few fools left.
> *Algernon.* We have.
> *Jack.* I should extremely like to meet them. What do they
> talk about?
> *Algernon.* The fools? Oh! about the clever people, of
> course.
> *Jack.* What fools! [*Earnest*, pp. 51–52]

Or again:

> *Algernon.* I am obliged to go up by the first train on
> Monday morning. I have a business appointment that
> I am anxious . . . to miss?

> *Cecily.* Couldn't you miss it anywhere but in London?
> *Algernon.* No: the appointment is in London. [*Earnest,*
>   p. 78]

Not all the play's wit is harmless, though. Some of it has
the potential to corrupt too, and this is especially true of
Algy's comments about marriage. "Divorces are made in
Heaven" (*Earnest,* p. 8), Algy remarks, then soon afterward
observes that "in married life three is company and two is
none" (*Earnest,* p. 22). In the mouth of Wotton, such comments would have had a disastrous effect on Dorian. In
Earnest, however, the comments are amusing but harmless.
They have no effect on Jack, to whom they are addressed, or
on Algy, who utters them. Both pursue the goal of marriage
in the play and end up happily married. At one point, Algy
repeats a famous epigram of Wotton's:

> *Algernon.* All women become like their mothers. That is
>   their tragedy. No man does. That's his.
> *Jack.* Is that clever?
> *Algernon.* It is perfectly phrased! and quite as true as any
>   observation in civilised life should be. [*Earnest,* p. 51]

In this brief exchange, Wilde concisely sums up his attitude
toward Wotton in *The Importance of Being Earnest.* Wotton's
corrupt, immoral epigrams are now seen as toothless. Wit
exists because it is perfectly phrased, and for no other reason.
The play is full of witty comments whose only purpose is to
be perfectly phrased and therefore highly amusing—wit for
wit's sake, so to speak.

In *The Picture of Dorian Gray,* Wotton existed literally as
a Victorian devil, a modern-day Satan. This is parodied when
Jack says of Lady Bracknell: "Never met such a Gorgon. . . .
I don't really know what a Gorgon is like, but I am quite
sure that Lady Bracknell is one. In any case, she is a monster
without being a myth, which is rather unfair. . . . I beg your
pardon, Algy, I suppose I shouldn't talk about your own aunt
in that way before you" (*Earnest,* pp. 49–50). The monster, we

are immediately reminded, is only our good friend Algy's aunt. It is all very funny and very absurd. And she is, after all, a harmless monster whose attempt to keep Jack and Gwendolyn apart fails.

When it first appeared, *The Picture of Dorian Gray* evoked a tremendous amount of hostile criticism in the press because of its immorality. Replying to one of his critics, Wilde wrote to the editor of the *St. James's Gazette:* "The sphere of art and the sphere of ethics are absolutely distinct and separate; and it is to the confusion between the two that we owe the appearance of Mrs Grundy, that amusing old lady who represents the only original form of humour that the middle classes of this country have been able to produce" (*Letters*, p. 257).

Mrs. Grundy was the Victorian comic personification of ultrarespectability. In *The Importance of Being Earnest,* the critics of *Dorian Gray* are humorously satirized in the person of the mentally short-sighted Miss Prism, who is really Wilde's version of Mrs. Grundy. When we first meet her, Prism is a stiff-necked and morally upright person convinced of Cecily's great need to study German grammar as a means of "improving" herself. Amusingly, Prism connects the study of German, geology, and political economy with ethical improvement—presumably because of the dry, ascetic nature of these subjects. She speaks in a stilted manner and utters only moral platitudes, but these are constantly undercut by Cecily. In the four-act version, Cecily makes a flippant observation at one point, and Miss Prism wonders where Cecily is getting such ideas from, since they are "certainly not to be found in any of the improving books that I have procured for you." [8]

It soon turns out that Prism has written a three-volume novel:

> *Miss Prism.* Do not speak slightingly of the three-volume novel, Cecily. I wrote one myself in earlier days.
> *Cecily.* Did you really, Miss Prism? How wonderfully

8. Oscar Wilde, *The Complete Works of Oscar Wilde*, ed. J. B. Foreman, p. 356. See note 7 above.

clever you are! I hope it did not end happily? I don't
like novels that end happily. They depress me so much.
Miss Prism. The good ended happily, and the bad un-
happily. That is what Fiction means. [*Earnest*, p. 71]

Miss Prism subscribes to the view that the function of art is to
preach morality. As soon as Dr. Chasuble appears on the scene,
however, she abandons the task of "improving" Cecily and
begins to pursue the rector. All her moral platitudes and the
preachings of her three-volume novel are dropped as she sur-
renders to her sexual drive. She tries to maintain a façade of
respectability, but this façade is hilariously shattered when she
obliquely tries to suggest to Chasuble that she is the best
woman for him:

Miss Prism. No married man is ever attractive except to
his wife.
Chasuble. And often, I've been told, not even to her.
Miss Prism. That depends on the intellectual sympathies
of the woman. Maturity can always be depended on.
Ripeness can be trusted. Young women are green. (*Dr.
Chasuble starts.*) I spoke horticulturally. My metaphor
was drawn from fruits. [*Earnest*, p. 84]

Prism attempts to turn a sexual relationship into one of "intellectual sympathies," but her metaphor betrays her real
intentions.

Toward the end of the play, the subject of Miss Prism's
novel crops up again and Lady Bracknell passes judgment on
it, calling it "a three-volume novel of more than usually revolt-
ing sentimentality" (*Earnest*, p. 175). This is the final word on
Prism's moral work of fiction; the final word on Prism herself
comes when Dr. Chasuble embraces her and she cries out enthusiastically, "At last!" The critics of *Dorian Gray* and their
moral airs were, after all, so much hypocritical nonsense.

A good deal of the fun in *The Importance of Being Earnest*
is directed against *Salome.* A huge Negro executioner brought
Iokanaan's head to Salome on a silver shield, and she lustfully

proceeded to feast upon it. This gruesome event is parodied when Lane brings Algernon some cucumber sandwiches on a salver, and he gluttonously devours them all and remains hungry. Algy's action is not quite proper, as the sandwiches were intended for Lady Bracknell. Far from being crushed between huge salvers, moreover, Algy lives to dine again, first at Willis's, then on muffins at Jack's country home.

In the four-act version of the play, Jack too has a huge appetite. Masquerading as Ernest in the city, he has run up a tremendous food bill at the Savoy—£762 14s. 2d., to be precise —and finally a bailiff appears at Jack's country home to arrest Mr. Ernest Worthing. Algy, who is Bunburying in the country as Ernest, finds himself in deep trouble and is almost carted off to Holloway prison, but Cecily intervenes, and finally Jack is persuaded to step in and rescue Algy by paying the bill he himself had really run up at the Savoy. So Salome's insatiable, hellish sexual appetite is reduced in *Earnest* to the level of mild gluttony. Whereas Salome meets death for yielding to her uncontrollable appetite, Jack and Algy both escape punishment in *Earnest*. Wilde dismisses Salome with a peal of laughter, declaring that her hunger was, after all, nonsense. She would have done better to order some cucumber sandwiches—or to have gone, perhaps, to Willis's or even the Savoy!

Iokanaan is also parodied in the play. He makes a charming reappearance in the figure of the Reverend Frederick Chasuble, doctor of divinity. Like Iokanaan, Dr. Chasuble is continually baptizing people:

> *Jack.* Ah! that reminds me, you mentioned christenings I think, Dr. Chasuble? I suppose you know how to christen all right? (*Dr. Chasuble looks astounded.*) I mean, of course, you are continually christening, aren't you?
>
> *Miss Prism.* It is, I regret to say, one of the Rector's most constant duties in this parish. I have often spoken to the poorer classes on the subject. But they don't seem to know what thrift is. [*Earnest,* p. 88]

The chief similarity between Iokanaan and Dr. Chasuble, however, is that they are both celibates whose slips of the tongue betray deep sexual longings. Miss Prism, who is in full pursuit of Chasuble throughout the play, calls him a "womanthrope," and he replies, in a stilted, scholarly manner: "Believe me, I do not deserve so neologistic a phrase. The precept as well as the practice of the Primitive Church was distinctly against matrimony" (*Earnest*, p. 83). Chasuble remains celibate by virtue of repressing his longing for Miss Prism, but his words continually betray him and reveal his true nature. For instance:

> *Chasuble.* I hope, Cecily, you are not inattentive.
> *Cecily.* Oh, I am afraid I am.
> *Chasuble.* That is strange. Were I fortunate enough to be Miss Prism's pupil, I would hang upon her lips. (*Miss Prism glares.*) I spoke metaphorically.—My metaphor was drawn from bees. Ahem! [*Earnest*, pp. 72–73]

A few lines later, Chasuble makes another slip of the tongue:

> *Chasuble.* I must not disturb Egeria and her pupil any longer.
> *Miss Prism.* Egeria? My name is Lætitia, Doctor.
> *Chasuble.* (*Bowing.*) A classical allusion, merely, drawn from the Pagan authors. I shall see you both no doubt at Evensong?
> *Miss Prism.* I think, dear Doctor, I will have a stroll with you. I find I have a headache after all, and a walk might do it good.
> *Chasuble.* With pleasure, Miss Prism, with pleasure. We might walk as far as the schools and back [*Earnest*, pp. 73–74]

Egeria was a nymph who was both the teacher and the lover of King Numa Pompilius. She is said to have inspired the religious reforms he introduced. Chasuble associates Miss

Prism with Egeria after having wished he were her pupil.
Immediately after that, he takes her for a walk to the schools.
And indeed, it is Chasuble rather than Cecily who is Prism's
real pupil, and Prism for whose sake he finally adandons both
the precept and the practice of the Primitive Church.
The canon's slips of the tongue are always amusing, as for
instance when Lady Bracknell begins to question him about
Prism:

> *Lady Bracknell.* Is this Miss Prism a female of repellent
> aspect, remotely connected with education?
> *Chasuble.* (*Somewhat indignantly.*) She is the most culti-
> vated of ladies, and the very picture of respectability.
> *Lady Bracknell.* It is obviously the same person. May I
> ask what position she holds in your household?
> *Chasuble.* (*Severely.*) I am a celibate, madam.
> *Jack.* (*Interposing.*) Miss Prism, Lady Bracknell, has been
> for the last three years Miss Cardew's esteemed gover-
> ness and valued companion.
> *Lady Bracknell.* In spite of what I hear of her, I must see
> her at once. Let her be sent for.
> *Chasuble.* (*Looking off.*) She approaches; she is nigh.
> (*Enter Miss Prism hurriedly.*) [*Earnest*, pp. 173–74]

In this scene Chasuble automatically misconstrues Lady
Bracknell's question and leaps to the defense of his chastity.
Jack, by interposing, undercuts the canon's reply and makes
his slip seem even more ridiculous. Then Chasuble proceeds
to announce the coming of Prism as though she were a divinity. Chasuble is very much like Iokanaan, but whereas Iokanaan was shrouded in an atmosphere of horror and evil,
Chasuble is a comic figure with a ridiculous lust for the
middle-aged, unattractive Prism. He is a reductio ad absurdum of Iokanaan. Unlike the prophet, he does not have to die
to possess his lover. He merely lowers his defenses and embraces the delighted Prism. All ends harmlessly and happily
for him.

A Woman of No Importance is ridiculed in a brief episode toward the end of act 3. Jack mistakenly falls under the impression that Prism is his mother and suddenly becomes ridiculously sentimental:

> *Jack.* (*In a pathetic voice.*) Miss Prism, more is restored to you than this hand-bag. I was the baby you placed in it.
> *Miss Prism.* (*Amazed.*) You?
> *Jack.* (*Embracing her.*) Yes . . . mother!
> *Miss Prism.* (*Recoiling in indignant astonishment.*) Mr. Worthing! I am unmarried!
> *Jack.* Unmarried! I do not deny that is a serious blow. But after all, who has the right to cast a stone against one who has suffered? Cannot repentance wipe out an act of folly? Why should there be one law for men, and another for women? Mother, I forgive you. (*Tries to embrace her again.*) [*Earnest,* pp. 179–80]

The blind sentimentalism of *A Woman of No Importance* is uproariously made fun of here. Behind the barrage of sentimentality in the former play had lurked the hideous leprosy of incest. This is ridiculed when Jack embraces Prism, for the embrace has clear and amusing sexual overtones. Miss Prism knows—and we immediately learn—that she is not Jack's mother. She recoils from his embrace, but he stupidly persists in trying to put his arms around his "mother."

Finally, in *An Ideal Husband,* Mrs. Cheveley lost a snake-bracelet and Lord Goring found it. When she tried to reclaim the bracelet, she was trapped, exposed as a thief, threatened with the police, and defeated. Similarly, Jack loses a cigarette-case and Algernon finds it. When Jack moves to reclaim his case, Algy discovers that Jack is "one of the most advanced Bunburyists" he knows. In one of the funniest episodes in *The Importance of Being Earnest,* Jack is trapped and exposed; but the result is that he gets his cigarette-case back and deepens his friendship with a fellow-Bunburyist. What had proved lethal for Mrs. Cheveley proves advantageous for Jack. Indeed, everything can be counted on to prove harmless in this never-never land of farce, Wilde's funniest and most delightful play.

Oscar Wilde was the type of subjective writer who always put himself into his works. He was later to write to Lord Douglas: "You knew what my Art was to me, the great primal note by which I had revealed, first myself to myself, and then myself to the world" (*Letters*, p. 447). Even this fact is parodied in *The Importance of Being Earnest*, when Cecily says of her diary: "It is simply a very young girl's record of her own thoughts and impressions, and consequently meant for publication" (*Earnest*, p. 104).

In 1887, Wilde had written in the *Pall Mall Gazette*: "A true artist, and such Rossetti undoubtedly was, reveals himself so perfectly in his work, that unless a biographer has something more valuable to give us than idle anecdotes and unmeaning tales, his labour is misspent and his industry misdirected." [9] If we apply this dictum to Wilde's own life, it would seem that he at first regarded the marquess of Queensberry as a joke. *The Importance of Being Earnest* was finished approximately six months before Wilde's court duels with Queensberry began, but during this interval he did not produce any literature. In the absence of literary proof to the contrary, it is fair to assume that Wilde maintained the mood of *Earnest* during these few months. Successful and relatively rich, there was no reason why he shouldn't have. Quite probably, he first went to court against Queensberry largely in a spirit of jovial indifference. The outcome was Wilde's conviction on charges of homosexuality and his sentencing to two years of hard labor. Suddenly, Oscar Wilde found himself imprisoned in a filthy hole dark as death

9. Oscar Wilde, *Reviews*, ed. Robert Ross, pp. 149–50. All future references to Wilde's reviews are to this edition and are cited in parentheses in the text. The edition will be designated as *Reviews*.

> And bound with bars lest Christ should see
> How men their brothers maim.[10]

The demon universe had yawned unexpectedly and swallowed
him up.

Or perhaps not so unexpectedly. Just before his imprisonment, Wilde had a chance to escape to the Continent, but he
did not. The reaction against the evil within oneself can take
many different forms, and Wilde's final reaction was to choose
external punishment.

10. Oscar Wilde, *The Ballad of Reading Gaol*. In Oscar Wilde, *Poems*,
ed. Robert Ross, p. 340, sect. 5. All future references to *The Ballad of
Reading Gaol* are to this edition and are cited in parentheses in the
text. The poem will be designated as *Gaol*. No line references are available in the edition, so I will give only the page reference and section number.

5 Hades and Finale

Everything to be true must become a religion.

WILDE, De Profundis

After his conviction for homosexuality, Wilde wrote *De Profundis* in prison and later, from the Continent, *The Ballad of Reading Gaol.* In both *The Picture of Dorian Gray* and *Salome,* Wilde had warned that a balance must be maintained when exploring the demon universe in life, and had shown the terrible consequences of not keeping such a balance. In *De Profundis,* he records his own loss of equilibrium:

> Tired of being on the heights I deliberately went to the depths in search for new sensations. What the paradox was to me in the sphere of thought, perversity became to me in the sphere of passion. Desire, at the end, was a malady, or a madness, or both. I took pleasure where it pleased me and passed on. . . . I ceased to be Lord over myself. I was no longer the Captain of my Soul, and did not know it. I allowed you to dominate me, and your father to frighten me. I ended in horrible disgrace. [*Letters,* p. 446]

Wilde compares his pursuit of perverse sensations in life to his love of the paradoxical in art. The paradox knows no middle ground, however, and Wilde continued to plunge deeper into the turbulent waters of sin until he lost control and was dragged to the bottom.

De Profundis—Ross's title and a good one—has the relationship between Oscar Wilde, Satan, and Christ for its main theme. A deeply terrifying and very moving piece, it records Wilde's futile attempt to free himself from the grip of Satan and to attain the lofty spiritual heights of Jesus Christ. The work is a literary autobiography, built carefully on the principle of counterpoint. Veiled in the form of a letter because this was all the prison authorities would allow Wilde to write, its chief fault is that in it Wilde yields too much to the epistolary impulse: the disguise becomes, at times, the reality. *De Profundis* is a unique work, however, for in it Wilde creates a private myth and sees his life entirely in terms of this myth. His Christ and his Satan are both private symbols:

> Religion does not help me. The faith that others give to what is unseen, I give to what one can touch, and look at. My Gods dwell in temples made with hands, and within the circle of actual experience is my creed made complete: too complete, it may be, for like many or all of those who have placed their Heaven in this earth, I have found in it not merely the beauty of Heaven, but the horror of Hell also. When I think about Religion at all, I feel as if I would like to found an order for those who cannot believe: the Confraternity of the Fatherless one might call it, where on an altar, on which no taper burned, a priest, in whose heart peace had no dwelling, might celebrate with unblessed bread and a chalice empty of wine. Everything to be true must become a religion. . . . But whether it be faith or agnosticism, it must be nothing external to me. Its symbols must be of my own creating. [*Letters*, p. 468]

In this lengthy passage, Wilde provides us with the key to a thorough understanding of *De Profundis*. Rejecting Christianity and locating both his heaven and his hell on this earth, he mythologizes his world, turning it into a fantastic religious universe. He creates for himself a private Satan—Lord Alfred Douglas—and a private Christ, devoid of supernatural attributes and seen as the supreme artist and the first Romantic. As he says, his religion springs from within himself and its symbols are of his own creating. A religion it is, however, and within its lonely framework Wilde will either be saved or damned.

De Profundis falls rather neatly into three structural parts. The first revolves around Satan and Wilde's relationship with him. "I discern in all our relations," Wilde says to Lord Alfred,

"not Destiny merely, but Doom: Doom that walks always swiftly, because she goes to the shedding of blood. Through your father you come of a race, marriage with whom is horrible, friendship fatal, and that lays violent hands either on its own life or on the lives of others. In every little circumstance in which the ways of our lives met; in every point of great, or seemingly trivial import in which you came to me for pleasure or for help; in the small scances, the slight accidents that look, in their relation to life, to be no more than the dust that dances in a beam, or the leaf that flutters from a tree, Ruin followed, like the echo of a bitter cry, or the shadow that hunts with the beast of prey." [*Letters*, p. 440]

The consistent use of demonic imagery to characterize Douglas and his father is by no means a form of rhetorical exaggeration. Wilde deliberately builds them up as the Satan-figures of his private religion, though the father remains somewhat secondary, as Lord Alfred occupies and monopolizes the foreground. Wilde says to Alfred: "I should have shaken you out of my life as a man shakes from his raiment a thing that has stung him. . . . Æschylus tells us of the great Lord who brings up in his house the lion-cub, . . . and loves it because it comes bright-eyed to his call and fawns on him for its food. . . . And the thing grows up and shows the nature of its race, . . . and destroys the lord and his house and all that he possesses. I feel that I was such a one as he" (*Letters*, p. 431). After reading one of Douglas's letters, Wilde says he "felt almost polluted, as though by associating with one of such a nature I had soiled and shamed my life irretrievably" (*Letters*, p. 439). He refers to Douglas's "sudden fits of almost epileptic rage," to "those incessant scenes that seemed to be almost physically necessary to you, and in which your mind and body grew distorted and you became a thing as terrible to look at as to listen to" (*Letters*, p. 429).

Indeed, Wilde asserts that only Lord Alfred and his father were ever able to inspire genuine terror in him. Here is one of his quarrels with Alfred, as Wilde lay ill and suffering from a high fever:

> I told you at length to leave the room: you pretended to do so, but when I lifted up my head from the pillow in which I had buried it, you were still there, and with brutality of laughter and hysteria of rage you moved suddenly towards me. A sense of horror came over me, for what exact reason I could not make out; but I got out of my bed at once, and bare-footed and just as I was, made my way down the two flights of stairs to the sitting-room, which I did not leave until the owner of the lodgings—whom I had rung for—had assured me that you had left my bedroom, and promised to remain within call, in case of necessity. . . .
>
> Only once before in my life had I experienced such a feeling of horror at any human being. It was when in my library at Tite Street, waving his small hands in the air in epileptic fury, your father, with his bully, or his friend, between us, had stood uttering every foul word his foul mouth could think of, and screaming the loathsome threats he afterwards with such cunning carried out. [*Letters*, pp. 437–38]

What astonishes Wilde is that Alfred is not the mythical Satan himself but only a human being. Lord Alfred, however, turns out to be Wilde's private Satan, his enemy—"such an enemy as no man ever had" (*Letters*, p. 452). "Out of the dust of the common highway that the hooves of horned things pash into mire you have moulded your perfect semblance for me to look at" (*Letters*, p. 464), he tells Douglas, holding up to him a mirror that reflects the hideous, unmasked face of Satan.

The chief qualities of Lord Alfred Douglas are the exact

opposites of those Wilde attributes to his Christ. Although he has the rudiments of an artistic nature, Douglas is isolated from the beauties of art. His influence on Wilde's art is purely destructive:

> While you were with me you were the absolute ruin of my Art, and in allowing you to stand persistently between Art and myself I give to myself shame and blame in the fullest degree. You couldn't know, you couldn't understand, you couldn't appreciate. I had no right to expect it of you at all. Your interests were merely in your meals and moods. Your desires were simply for amusements, for ordinary or less ordinary pleasures. They were what your temperament needed, or thought it needed for the moment. [*Letters*, p. 427]

Douglas was delighted by the brilliant successes of Wilde's first nights, by the banquets that followed them, by the fact that he was the intimate friend of a distinguished artist; but he "could not understand the conditions requisite for the production of artistic work." As a consequence, his influence on Wilde was to blast and destroy the latter's artistic impulse: "Whether at Torquay, Goring, London, Florence or elsewhere, my life, as long as you were by my side, was entirely sterile and uncreative" (*Letters*, p. 426).

Douglas is a selfish, insolent, narrow, and unimaginative person, remote from art, but these qualities of his only serve to indicate to us his most basic and terrifying quality—hate. Wilde traces all of Douglas's personality characteristics to this single hellish source: "Hate so blinded you that you could see no further than the narrow, walled-in, and already lust-withered garden of your common desires. Your terrible lack of imagination, the one really fatal defect of your character, was entirely the result of the Hate that lived in you. Subtly, silently, and in secret, Hate gnawed at your nature, as the lichen bites at the root of some sallow plant, till you grew to see nothing but the most meagre interests and the most petty aims" (*Letters*, p. 445).

Later on, he says to him, further underlining the point: "Hate, you have yet to learn, is, intellectually considered, the Eternal Negation. Considered from the point of view of the emotions it is a form of Atrophy, and kills everything but itself" (*Letters*, p. 450). Douglas's hate, moreover, is directed against his father: "Your hatred of your father was of such stature that it entirely outstripped, o'erthrew, and overshadowed your love of me. There was no struggle between them at all, or but little; of such dimensions was your hatred and of such monstrous growth. . . . There was not a glass of champagne you drank, not a rich dish you ate of in all these years, that did not feed your Hate and make it fat" (*Letters*, p. 445).

It is worth noting at this stage that *De Profundis* is about the past, the present, and the future. Wilde stresses this at the very beginning of the piece, when he says he will write "of the past and of the future, of sweet things changed to bitterness and of bitter things that may be turned into joy" (*Letters*, p. 424), and will write from the midnight loneliness of Reading Gaol. It is important to realize, moreover, that when Wilde writes of the past, he attempts—like Wordsworth in *The Prelude* but less successfully—both to recreate experience and to analyze it from the vantage point of the present.

From Reading Gaol, Wilde sees Douglas as a Satan-figure, and feels only bitterness and scorn for him. Earlier, in happier days, he had seen him as a weak person, felt sympathy for him, and forgiven him his weaknesses. These two attitudes exist side by side as Wilde reviews the past, and—since *De Profundis* is largely an unpolished first draft[1]—they some-

---

1. In April, 1897, Major Nelson, then governor of Reading Gaol, reported to the prison commissioners explaining how *De Profundis* had been written: "Each sheet was carefully numbered before being issued and withdrawn each evening at locking and placed before me in the morning with the usual papers." Mr. Rupert Hart-Davis, however, argues quite convincingly that Major Nelson was more charitable to Wilde than his official position allowed him to admit. Nevertheless, thé extent of Major Nelson's considerateness must not be overestimated. Each sheet may not have been withdrawn every evening, and Wilde may have been allowed to make fair copies of sheets 1, 2, and 13, but *De Profundis* re-

times lead to confusion and seeming contradiction. There is no contradiction, however. It was precisely this inability to recognize Douglas as a Satan-figure until too late that led to Wilde's downfall. Out of sympathy for Douglas, Wilde had drifted into the habit of yielding to him in small things. As a result, his will-power became entirely subject to Douglas's and he was unable to withdraw when Douglas revealed himself as a hate-filled, Satanic person and reached out for Wilde's soul, desiring to use it as a weapon against the elder Douglas:

> Having made your own of my genius, my will-power and my fortune, you required, in the blindness of an inexhaustible greed, my entire existence. You took it. . . . Blindly I staggered as an ox into the shambles. I had made a gigantic psychological error. I had always thought that my giving up to you in small things meant nothing: that when a great moment arrived I could reassert my will-power in its natural superiority. It was not so. At the great moment my will-power completely failed me. In life there is really no small or great thing. All things are of equal value and of equal size. My habit—due to indifference chiefly at first—of giving up to you in everything had become insensibly a real part of my nature. Without my knowing it, it had stereotyped my temperament to one permanent and fatal mood. [*Letters*, pp. 429–30]

Wilde observes bitterly that he had become, against his will, a weapon with which Douglas and his father fought each other:

> You thought simply of how to get your father into prison. To see him "in the dock," as you used to say; that was your one idea. . . . Well, you had your desire gratified. Hate granted you every single thing you wished for.

mains largely a first draft written under exacting circumstances. For Mr. Hart-Davis's argument, see *Letters*, p. 423, n. 2.

It was an indulgent Master to you. It is so, indeed, to all who serve it. For two days you sat on a high seat with the Sheriffs, and feasted your eyes with the spectacle of your father standing in the dock of the Central Criminal Court. And on the third day I took his place. What had occurred? In your hideous game of hate together, you had both thrown dice for my soul, and you happened to have lost. That was all. [*Letters,* pp. 447–48]

Douglas, quite carelessly, had staked Wilde's soul against Queensberry's, but the roll of the dice had gone against him. The dice game over, Wilde—disgraced, ruined, and abandoned—was cast into a hell where "suffering is one long moment," where "time itself does not progress. It revolves. It seems to circle round one centre of pain" (*Letters,* p. 457).

This external hell, moreover, created a corresponding hell within the self:

Prison-life, with its endless privations and restrictions, makes one rebellious. The most terrible thing about it is not that it breaks one's heart—hearts are made to be broken—but that it turns one's heart to stone. One sometimes feels that it is only with a front of brass and a lip of scorn that one can get through the day at all. And he who is in a state of rebellion cannot receive grace, to use the phrase of which the Church is so fond—so rightly fond, I dare say—for in life, as in Art, the mood of rebellion closes up the channels of the soul, and shuts the airs of heaven." [*Letters,* pp. 474–75]

It is the hell within that Wilde, Prometheus-like, seeks to destroy in *De Profundis.* He tries to do this by developing beyond bitterness and rebellion, and it is very important to recognize that he feels he must do so while still in prison: "Though at present you may find it a thing hard to believe, it is true none the less that for you, living in freedom and idleness and comfort, it is more easy to learn the lessons of Humility than it is for me, who begin the day by going down on my knees and washing the floor of my cell. . . . Yet I *must learn*

these lessons here, if I am to learn them anywhere" (*Letters,*
pp. 474–75; italics mine).

The second part of *De Profundis* revolves around Christ
and Wilde's relationship with him. It consists of a lengthy
transition and a long section on Jesus, and begins when Wilde
says to Douglas: "And the end of it all is that I have got to
forgive you. I must do so. I don't write this letter to put bitterness into your heart, but to pluck it out of mine. For my own
sake I must forgive you" (*Letters,* p. 465). A while later, he
adds: "My nature is seeking a fresh mode of self-realisation.
That is all I am concerned with. And the first thing that I
have got to do is to free myself from any possible bitterness
of feeling against you" (*Letters,* p. 467). This, then, is going to
be the test of Wilde's success or failure in his attempt to rise
from the depths. If he cannot destroy the bitterness and hatred
within himself, he will remain in hell long after the prison
gates have opened and he has emerged into the fresh air and
sunshine.

The basic underlying theme of *De Profundis* is a familiar
one. It is none other than the theme of the fairy tales, especially "The Young King." Like the young king, Wilde had
begun his life by devoting himself entirely to pleasure, but
had fallen into a demon universe of pain and guilt. At the onset of his life, he tells us, he determined to eat of the fruit of
all the trees in the garden of the world; but he made the
mistake of confining himself exclusively "to the trees of what
seemed to me the sun-gilt side of the garden, and shunned the
other side for its shadow and its gloom":

> Failure, disgrace, poverty, sorrow, despair, suffering,
> tears even, the broken words that come from the lips of
> pain, remorse that makes one walk in thorns, conscience
> that condemns, self-abasement that punishes, the misery
> that puts ashes on its head, the anguish that chooses sack-
> cloth for its raiment and into its own drink puts gall—all
> these were things of which I was afraid. And as I had
> determined to know nothing of them, I was forced to

taste each one of them in turn, to feed on them, to have
for a season, indeed, no other food at all. [*Letters,* p. 475]

Whereas the young king came in contact with the demon
universe largely through dreams, however, Wilde's fall was
merciless in its severity—and another fairy tale, "The Star-
Child," shows what a too severe fall into the demon universe
can do to a person. At any rate, the young king united all opposites and attained a state of higher innocence through
Christ, and Wilde aspires to do the same in *De Profundis:*
"This new life, as through my love of Dante I like sometimes
to call it, is, of course, no new life at all, but simply the con-
tinuance, by means of development, and evolution, of my
former life" (*Letters,* p. 475). As in the later fairy tales, the
movement from innocence into the demon universe is seen as
only part of the development toward a higher innocence that
fuses all opposites in love. The great danger, however, is that
this evolution may be arrested:

> The important thing, the thing that lies before me, the
> thing that I have to do, or be for the brief remainder of
> my days one maimed, marred, and incomplete, is to ab-
> sorb into my nature all that has been done to me, to make
> it part of me, to accept it without complaint, fear, or re-
> luctance. The supreme vice is shallowness. Whatever is
> realised is right.
>
>   .   .   .   .
>
> To reject one's own experiences is to arrest one's own
> development. To deny one's own experiences is to put a
> lie into the lips of one's own life. It is no less than a
> denial of the Soul. [*Letters,* p. 469]

To reject the demon universe, to rise up against it in hate
and bitterness, is to perpetuate it within the self. Experiencing
the demonic world is a necessary step in the development toward a higher innocence that will absorb and reconcile all opposites within an all-encompassing framework of love.
The Christ Wilde worships in *De Profundis* is a secular and

more elaborate version of the Christ the young king kneeled before. It is worth observing, though, that Wilde's Christ is not an entirely private symbol but is rooted in *Sartor Resartus* and in late nineteenth-century attitudes. Carlyle, in *Sartor Resartus,* exalted Christ as an artist and identified him as "the higher Orpheus." Wilde knew *Sartor Resartus* quite well and requested and received a copy of it while in prison. In *De Profundis,* moreover, he states that his mother knew Carlyle in person,[2] and mentions this only a few pages before he places Christ among the poets. It is quite probable, therefore, that Wilde's Christ has his origins in Carlyle's book.

The secularization of Christ in *De Profundis* is also not original. Toward the end of the nineteenth century, Christianity had crumbled as a religion for the educated mind and intellectuals were trying to salvage the teachings of Christ while dismissing the miracles. George Bernard Shaw's attitude toward Christ in the preface to *Major Barbara* is typical. Thomas Hardy's attitude is also typical—a deep respect for Christ coupled with moody atheism. Wilde, in viewing the gospels as prose-poems and explaining the miracles away as forms of poetic hyperbole, fits within the intellectual pattern of the period. For him Christ, though unique, is a man, no more supernatural than Douglas.

Wilde's great original idea is his identification of Christ as the first Romantic. The three major intellectual currents in nineteenth-century England were Romanticism, orthodox Christianity, and scientific rationalism. In *De Profundis* Wilde is Romantic in the fullest sense of the word, but his favorite Romantic is not Wordsworth, Blake, or Shelley, but Christ. The Romantics were vague and mystical in their religion, but through the imagination they sought to blend all opposites, reach the universal spirit, and transform the entire life of man. Christ was far more successful than Wordsworth, Blake, and the other Romantics in these endeavors. Wilde kneels before him as the supreme Romantic, whose life was an ex-

2. See *Letters,* p. 472. Wilde speaks of a book Carlyle had given his mother years before.

tremely wonderful poem, an exquisite idyll. If Wilde can turn his own life into a similar poem, then he will have entered heaven through Christ, as he entered hell through Douglas. Whereas Wilde saw Douglas's nature as antithetical to art, he sees Christ's nature as that of the supreme artist, despite the fact that Douglas actually wrote some poetry while Christ never produced any art: "I remember saying once to André Gide, as we sat together in some Paris café, that while Metaphysics had but little real interest for me, and Morality absolutely none, there was nothing that either Plato or Christ had said that could not be transferred immediately into the sphere of Art, and there find its complete fulfilment." Christ, he goes on, "realised in the entire sphere of human relations that imaginative sympathy which in the sphere of Art is the sole secret of creation" (*Letters*, p. 476).

While Douglas was unimaginative, Christ has an intense and flamelike imagination: "It is the imaginative quality of Christ's own nature that makes him this palpitating centre of romance. The strange figures of poetic drama and ballad are made by the imagination of others, but out of his own imagination entirely did Jesus of Nazareth create himself" (*Letters*, p. 482).

Douglas was imprisoned within the narrow, lustful bounds of his ego, but Christ is associated with the boundless and the infinite. His nature, in its Romantic intensity, goes beyond all limitations and rejects all fragmentation, uniting opposites in a vision of total harmony:

> Christ's place is indeed with the poets. His whole conception of Humanity sprang right out of the imagination and can only be realised by it. What God was to the Pantheist, man was to him. He was the first to conceive the divided races as a unity. Before his time there had been gods and men. He alone saw that on the hills of life there were but God and Man, and, feeling through the mysticism of sympathy that in himself each had been made incarnate, he calls himself the Son of the One or the son of the other, according to his mood. [*Letters*, p. 477]

To break the bonds of the ego and unite with the outer and transcendent worlds in a harmonious synthesis is the very essence of Romanticism—the ultimate experience, which the Romantic poets usually referred to as "Joy," and which they asserted only the imaginative faculty can attain. Christ, then, is not only the first but also the most successful Romantic, for he reached this state of Joy and maintained it throughout his life. His nature could not accept fragmentation and narrowness, so his imagination embraced God and he attained a wholly synthetic vision.

Whereas Douglas was insolent, selfish, and cruel, Christ is a mild, generous, and sympathetic person. But all of Christ's qualities are traceable to a single, wonderful source—love: "And while in reading the Gospels—particularly that of St John himself, or whatever early Gnostic took his name and mantle—I see this continual assertion of the imagination as the basis of all spiritual and material life, I see also that to Christ imagination was simply a form of Love, and that to him Love was Lord in the fullest meaning of the phrase" (*Letters* p. 484).

It is out of this single fundamental source that Christ's scintillating imagination sprang into being, bringing with it all the wonders of a godlike personality. Wilde hammers the point home: "The imagination is simply a manifestation of Love, and it is love, and the capacity for it, that distinguishes one human being from another" (*Letters,* p. 486). If capacity for love is what distinguishes human beings from one another, then Douglas and Christ stand as explicit opposites. The former has a totally hate-blasted personality, while the latter's nature overflows with love. The final and most basic opposition in *De Profundis* is that between hate and love.

The young king rose from before the image of Christ a regenerated person, and his story ended there. *De Profundis* is not a fairy tale, however, and Wilde rises from kneeling before his Christ full of bitterness and hate. The final section of *De Profundis*—which begins where all mention of Christ ends—gradually becomes more and more bitter until the emotion

of hate engulfs everything and Wilde again starts to lash out
mercilessly at Lord Alfred. In a scathing attack, Wilde reduces
Douglas to diminutive proportions: "You forced your way
into a life too large for you, one whose orbit transcended your
power of vision no less than your power of cyclic motion, one
whose thoughts, passions and actions were of intense import,
of wide interest, and fraught, too heavily indeed, with wonderful or awful consequence. Your little life of little whims
and moods was admirable in its own little sphere" (Letters,
p. 503).

There is infinite contempt in the constant repetition of the
word little. Wilde's haughty attribution of largeness to himself, moreover, shows that he has not yet even begun to learn
the lessons of humility. The hell within has not been destroyed, Douglas has not been forgiven. The attack continues, growing more and more bitter, and Douglas's littleness
becomes the measure of Wilde's inability to weed out of his
soul the terrible emotion of hate:

> Deliberately and by me uninvited you thrust yourself
> into my sphere, usurped there a place for which you had
> neither right nor qualifications, and having by curious
> persistence . . . succeeded in absorbing my entire life,
> could do no better with that life than break it in pieces.
> . . . If one gives to a child a toy too wonderful for its
> little mind, or too beautiful for its but half-awakened
> eyes, it breaks the toy, if it is wilful; if it is listless it lets it
> fall and goes its way to its own companions. So it was with
> you. Having got hold of my life, you did not know what
> to do with it. You couldn't have known. It was too won-
> derful a thing to be in your grasp. You should have let it
> slip from your hands and gone back to your own com-
> panions at their play. But unfortunately you were wilful,
> and so you broke it. [Letters, pp. 505–06]

Not even Douglas's mother—by Wilde's own account a
gentle and timid creature—is spared: "You will ask me in
what way your mother contributed to my destruction. I will

tell you. Just as you strove to shift on to me all your immoral
responsibilities, so your mother strove to shift on to me all her
moral responsibilities with regard to you. Instead of speaking
directly to you about your life, as a mother should, she always
spoke privately to me with earnest, frightened entreaties not
to let you know that she was writing to me. You see the position in which I was placed between you and your mother. It
was one as false, as absurd, and as tragic as the one in which I
was placed between you and your father" (*Letters*, p. 496).

This final section is Wilde's confession that he has been unable to destroy the bitterness and hate within himself. The
basic, pulsing emotion within his heart is hate, not love. At
the very end of *De Profundis,* he gives prison life as the reason
for his failure to purify himself: "How far I am from the true
temper of soul, this letter in its changing, uncertain moods, its
scorn and bitterness, *its aspirations and its failure to realise
those aspirations,* shows you quite clearly. But do not forget
in what a terrible school I am sitting at my task" (*Letters,*
p. 511; italics mine). When Wilde wrote these sentences, the
gates of Reading Gaol—the terrible school—were about to be
opened for him in two months' time. This explains why a note
of hope resounds through the final pages of *De Profundis.*

Once he is released from his external hell, Wilde believes,
the hell within may be easier to destroy. He presents a detailed plan of purification whose final stage will be the acceptance of Douglas in love. On his release, Wilde will give
himself entirely over to the beauties of nature for a while, for
this will cleanse and purify his soul:

> Society, as we have constituted it, will have no place for
> me, has none to offer; but Nature, whose sweet rains fall
> on unjust and just alike, will have clefts in the rocks
> where I may hide, and secret valleys in whose silence I
> may weep undisturbed. She will hang the night with stars
> so that I may walk abroad in the darkness without stum-
> bling, and send the wind over my footprints so that none
> may track me to my hurt: she will cleanse me in great

waters, and with bitter herbs make me whole. [*Letters,* p. 510]

During this period, Wilde hopes to have the ultimate Wordsworthian experience of uniting with the universal spirit that manifests itself in the forms of nature: "I am conscious now that behind all this Beauty, satisfying though it be, there is some Spirit hidden of which the painted forms are but modes of manifestation, and it is with this Spirit that I desire to become in harmony" (*Letters,* p. 509). He will also be living abroad by the sea—for the sea "washes away the stains and wounds of the world"—and he will be accompanied by Robert Ross and More Adey, his friends. At the end of this stage, which will take approximately one month, he hopes to have gained "peace, and balance, and a less troubled heart, and a sweeter mood" (*Letters,* p. 509).

Then will come a second and more difficult stage. He will meet Douglas in forgiveness and love. When Wilde's heart becomes large enough to embrace the Satanic Lord Douglas in love, he will have attained a Christlike state of total purity. Wilde describes this second stage:

> At the end of the month, when the June roses are in all their wanton opulence, I will, if I feel able, arrange through Robbie to meet you in some quiet foreign town like Bruges, whose grey houses and green canals and cool still ways had a charm for me, years ago. . . .
>
> I hope that our meeting will be what a meeting between you and me should be, after everything that has occurred. In old days there was always a wide chasm between us, the chasm of achieved Art and acquired culture: there is a still wider chasm between us now, the chasm of Sorrow: but to Humility there is nothing that is impossible, and to Love all things are easy. [*Letters,* p. 510]

The plan is an admirable one, but Wilde's complete failure to move out of his internal hell while still in prison augurs ill for his success after the prison gates open. Artistically, too, the

divided aim of *De Profundis*—it is both a letter and a literary
autobiography—suggests that Wilde has lost the single-minded
determination necessary for the production of great art. The
fact that *De Profundis* is largely an unpolished first draft does
not excuse its heavily epistolary nature. Furthermore, Wilde
could have revised it after his release, but he left it as it was,
perhaps out of indifference, but possibly because he felt that
its very weaknesses had their significance. After all, one of the
main themes of *De Profundis* is that hate isolates a person
from art. Douglas, hate-filled, knows nothing of art, and the
weakest parts of *De Profundis*—those which read most like a
letter—are those in which Wilde expresses his hatred for
Douglas.

Oscar Wilde was released from prison on the nineteenth of
May, 1897, and in less than two weeks he had already begun
The Ballad of Reading Gaol. The poem was written in June,
July, and August of 1897, but Wilde continued to revise it for
two more months and finally had it printed by Leonard
Smithers at the Chiswick Press under the pseudonym C.3.3.,
his cell number.

Wilde knew that society would have no place for him after
his emergence from prison. What he did not know was that
the Church would also reject him. This is evinced by the fact
that in *De Profundis* he speaks of Christ's love for the sinner
and of the sinner's repentance as his moment of initiation—
the moment in which he realizes what he has done, and
thereby alters his past. Ada Leverson, Wilde's close friend,
tells how, the morning after his release, he wrote to a Roman
Catholic retreat, asking if he might retire there for six months
(apparently he preferred this path of self-purification to the
one described at the end of *De Profundis*). He then waited
for the reply:

"Do you know one of the punishments that happen to
people who have been 'away'? They are not allowed to
read *The Daily Chronicle!* Coming along I begged to be

allowed to read it on the train. 'No!' Then I suggested I might be allowed to read it upside down. This they consented to allow, and I read all the way *The Daily Chronicle* upside down, and never enjoyed it so much. It's really the only way to read newspapers."

The man returned with the letter. We all looked away as Oscar read it. They replied that they could not accept him in the Retreat at the impulse of the moment. It must be thought over for at least a year. In fact they refused him.

Then he broke down and sobbed bitterly.[3]

That road to self-purification had been blocked for him.

The Ballad of Reading Gaol is a deeply moving generalization about the human situation from personal experience. Again, Wilde mythologizes his world and turns it into a religious universe, and again the religion is a private one springing primarily from within the self. The poem's main theme is that every man, sometime during his life, commits an act so vile that he isolates himself forever from "God's sweet world" and damns himself to a hell from which there is no escape. The poem dramatizes Reading Gaol as the abyss, the bottomless pit of a hell-on-earth, presenting it as a symbolic prison, a place for sinners who have been cast out of God's universe. Its inhabitants are the damned and its gates will never be opened.

A chief fault of the poem, however, is that Wilde sometimes treats Reading Gaol not as a God-created hell for sinners but as a human crime against God's mercy. Thus the poem has two irreconcilable themes. though the dominant one is definitely that of damnation. *The Ballad of Reading Gaol* is really a prolonged wail of despair from a person who finds himself permanently damned. In it, Wilde declares his inability to depart from his two-fold hell—the external hell

3. In Ada Leverson, *Letters to the Sphinx from Oscar Wilde, with Reminiscences of the Author* (1930). Quoted in *Letters*, p. 564.

of punishment and the internal hell of spiritual foulness—
even after he has become a free man, and declares that such
an escape will never occur. He will remain trapped in hell
until death annihilates him.

To understand *The Ballad of Reading Gaol*, we must first
recognize that it is meant to counterpoint another famous
ballad, written at the beginning of the century—*The Rime
of the Ancient Mariner*. At times, Wilde's ballad clearly
echoes Coleridge's:

> They glided past, they glided fast,
>   Like travellers through a mist:
> They mocked the moon in a rigadoon
>   Of delicate turn and twist,
> And with formal pace and loathsome grace
>   The phantoms kept their tryst.
>
> With mop and mow, we saw them go,
>   Slim shadows hand in hand:
> About, about, in ghostly rout
>   They trod a saraband:
> And the damned grotesques made arabesques,
>   Like the wind upon the sand!
>   [*Gaol*, p. 329, sect. 3]

Place these two stanzas for a moment beside a stanza from
The Rime of the Ancient Mariner and the similarity becomes
obvious:

> About, about, in reel and rout
> The death-fires danced at night;
> The water, like a witch's oils,
> Burnt green, and blue and white.
>   [ll. 127–30]

Wilde is not indulging in mere imitation, however, when he
hauntingly echoes Coleridge's ballad and practically lifts one
of his lines. What he is doing, rather, is forcing us to remember *The Rime of the Ancient Mariner* and therefore to com-

pare and contrast these two ballads that stand at opposite ends
of the nineteenth century.

There is a good deal of similarity between the guardsman
of *The Ballad of Reading Gaol* and the ancient mariner. The
guardsman, like the mariner, commits an act of murder and
thereby isolates himself from God and plunges himself into
hell—an external hell of punishment and an internal one of
spiritual anguish and depravity. The poem begins with
Wilde reporting the murder to us:

> He did not wear his scarlet coat,
>   For blood and wine are red,
> And blood and wine were on his hands
>   When they found him with the dead,
> The poor dead woman whom he loved,
>   And murdered in her bed.
>   [*Gaol,* p. 315, sect. 1]

The ancient mariner shot the albatross for no apparent
reason, and it is important to note that the guardsman, too,
has no motive for his crime. We are told that he loved the
woman he killed, and any hint of her possible faithlessness is
dispelled by the word *poor.* The crime is presented simply as
a drunken, mindless act. In a letter to Carlos Blacker on
August 4, 1897, Wilde wrote: "Why is it that one runs to
one's ruin? Why has destruction such a fascination? Why, when
one stands on a pinnacle, must one throw oneself down? No
one knows, but things are so" (*Letters,* p. 629).

Things are indeed so, for every man, we are told, kills the
thing he loves:

> Yet each man kills the thing he loves,
>   By each let this be heard,
> Some do it with a bitter look,
>   Some with a flattering word,
> The coward does it with a kiss,
>   The brave man with a sword!

Some kill their love when they are young,
And some when they are old;
Some strangle with the hands of Lust,
Some with the hands of Gold:
The kindest use a knife, because
The dead so soon grow cold.
[*Gaol*, pp. 316–17, sect. 1]

The guardsman, then, is no different from any other human
being, and his fate is symbolic of the human condition. It is
simply that he has committed an extreme act of sin and will
have to pay an extreme penalty. He will have to face the
ultimate horror of Reading Gaol—the hangman's noose. Section 1 ends with a lengthy reverie on the horror of being
hanged, presented in negations. Every man kills the thing he
loves, we are told; yet every man is not hanged by a terrible
group of grotesques:

He does not rise in piteous haste
To put on convict-clothes,
While some coarse-mouthed Doctor gloats, and notes
Each new and nerve-twitched pose,
Fingering a watch whose little ticks
Are like horrible hammer-blows.

He does not know that sickening thirst
That sands one's throat, before
The hangman with his gardener's gloves
Slips through the padded door,
And binds one with three leathern thongs,
That the throat may thirst no more.
[*Gaol*, p. 318, sect. 1]

The mariner's thirst is quenched by a cleansing, purifying
rain, but the guardsman will be released from his thirst only
when his neck snaps.

Wilde's ballad is a shocked and horror-filled repudiation of
Coleridge's view of the human situation in *The Rime of the*

Ancient Mariner. The mariner killed "a Christian soul" (l. 65) and fell into the demon universe as a result. After a period of terrible suffering, however, he had been reconciled with God. The mariner's punishment never totally ends—one is forever responsible for his deeds in life—but he is reconciled with God and we last meet him going into a church. For the guardsman, no such reconciliation is possible. His fall from grace is permanent, and he looks "wistfully" at God's world of beautiful blue skies and free, wandering clouds, yearning for it but with no real hope of ever again becoming part of it.

Wilde, moreover, wrote *The Ballad of Reading Gaol* largely in a stark, realistic style in order to impress us fully with the horror of hell. A fantastic, decorative style, which he yields to in parts of the ballad, would have shown us this hell only as one sees phantoms in a crystal. In an already quoted passage from *The Decay of Lying,* Wilde had stated that art in its second stage "keeps between herself and reality the impenetrable barrier of beautiful style, of decorative or ideal treatment" (*Intentions,* p. 22). Coleridge retains this impenetrable barrier between the reader and the demon universe in *The Rime of the Ancient Mariner,* but Wilde for the most part knocks it down in *The Ballad of Reading Gaol,* preferring instead to write in the grisly style of Thomas Hood's *The Dream of Eugene Aram, the Murderer.* Indeed, Hood's ballad is a major stylistic influence on Wilde's poem. Wilde, in rejecting his usual style, found himself forced to lean heavily on Hood, and he borrowed from *Eugene Aram* not only its stanza form but also its atmosphere and its uncompromisingly realistic presentation of a terrible theme.

In section 2, Wilde reports in dull amazement the movements of the man who has to swing. He also indulges in some serious punning. For instance:

> He did not wring his hands nor weep,
>   Nor did he peek or pine,
> But he drank the air as though it held
>   Some healthful anodyne;

> With open mouth he drank the sun
> As though it had been wine!
> [*Gaol*, p. 321, sect. 2]

The reference to wringing reminds us that the guardsman's neck is going to be wrung. He drinks the sun like wine, but it was precisely the wine he drank and spattered all over himself that led him mindlessly to kill the woman he loved. Nature—the symbol of God's world in the poem—does contain a healthful anodyne, but not for the damned. For the guardsman, the only real contact with nature will be the gallows-tree and its adder-bitten root, and he can only look "wistfully" at its other forms. The hope of *De Profundis*—that nature can heal and purify a sin-befouled soul—is rejected here.

The serious puns become more pronounced as the section moves on:

> It is sweet to dance to violins
> When Love and Life are fair:
> To dance to flutes, to dance to lutes
> Is delicate and rare:
> But it is not sweet with nimble feet
> To dance upon the air!
> [*Gaol*, p. 322, sect. 2]

The mood of the section is one of sick, dull reverie, and the puns serve to underscore the speaker's numbed sense of pain. So dazed and shocked is he, that terror and wit blend in his account of the doomed man. The section ends with Wilde identifying himself with the guardsman:

> Like two doomed ships that pass in a storm
> We had crossed each other's way:
> But we made no sign, we said no word,
> We had no word to say;
> For we did not meet in the holy night,
> But in the shameful day.

A prison wall was round us both,
Two outcast men we were:
The world had thrust us from its heart,
And God from out His care:
And the iron gin that waits for Sin
Had caught us in its snare.
[*Gaol,* p. 323, sect. 2]

The two men are identical in that they are both sinners thrust
out of God's universe. There is a profound difference between
them, however, as section 3 makes clear.

Section 3 of *The Ballad of Reading Gaol* reverses the basic
situation of the corresponding section of *The Rime of the
Ancient Mariner.* In the third section of Coleridge's poem,
the mariner is claimed by Life-in-Death while his shipmates
are claimed by Death. As they die one after the other, the
shipmates unload their burden of guilt on the mariner, turning him into a scapegoat. In *The Ballad of Reading Gaol,*
it is the guardsman who has to die, and Wilde and the inmates
voluntarily take upon themselves the burden of his guilt. The
guardsman realizes that death provides the only release from
his hellish existence, and he is happy to die:

He often said that he was glad
The hangman's hands were near.
[*Gaol,* p. 325, sect. 3]

Indeed, his sleep at the beginning of section 3 demonstrates
how glad he is and suggests the peace he will know when dead:

He lay as one who lies and dreams
In a pleasant meadow-land,
The watchers watched him as he slept,
And could not understand
How one could sleep so sweet a sleep
With a hangman close at hand.
[*Gaol,* p. 327, sect. 3]

As he slumbers, it is Wilde and the other inmates who feel
the terror and guilt of his sin:

> Alas! it is a fearful thing
>   To feel another's guilt!
> For, right within, the sword of Sin
>   Pierced to its poisoned hilt,
> And as molten lead were the tears we shed
>   For the blood we had not spilt.
>   [*Gaol*, p. 308, sect. 3]

The prisoners go down on their knees and pray for the guardsman, who is to be hanged at eight o'clock the next morning. Their prayers are unheard by God, however, who has cast them out of His universe, and are heard instead by evil sprites, who arrive and begin to torment them:

> Around, around, they waltzed and wound;
>   Some wheeled in smirking pairs;
> With the mincing step of a demirep
>   Some sidled up the stairs:
> And with subtle sneer, and fawning leer,
>   Each helped us at our prayers.
>   [*Gaol*, p. 330, sect. 3]

Finally, dawn comes and the stroke of eight approaches. The prisoners sit huddled in stony silence, their hearts beating madly with terror. Then the clock strikes eight and the guardsman is hanged, screaming once before he dies. For Wilde, whose existence is a life-in-death, the hanging holds more terror than it did for the guardsman:

> And as one sees some fearful things
>   In the crystal of a dream,
> We saw the greasy hempen rope
>   Hooked to the blackened beam,
> And heard the prayer the hangman's snare
>   Strangled into a scream.
>
> And all the woe that moved him so
>   That he gave that bitter cry,
> And the wild regrets, and the bloody sweats,
>   None knew so well as I:

> For he who lives more lives than one
> More deaths than one must die.
>   [*Gaol*, p. 330, sect. 3]

The guardsman gives one bitter cry and dies, but Wilde's
fate is far more terrible. He has to live on and die over and
over again. The emotions Wilde attributes to the guardsman
just before the hanging are largely Wilde's own feelings projected upon the doomed man, for—apart from a mumbled
prayer and the one scream—he has no way of knowing how
the guardsman felt.

Wilde begins section 4 by deepening the identification between the now-dead guardsman and the prisoners, himself
included. This is only the prelude to his revealing a terrible
truth, however. By sympathizing with the guardsman and tak-
ing upon their shoulders the burden of his guilt, the prisoners
have spiritually committed his crime over again:

> But there were those amongst us all
> Who walked with downcast head,
> And knew that, had each got his due,
> They would have died instead:
> He had but killed a thing that lived,
> Whilst they had killed the dead.

> For he who sins a second time
> Wakes a dead soul to pain,
> And draws it from its spotted shroud,
> And makes it bleed again,
> And makes it bleed great gouts of blood,
> And makes it bleed in vain!
>   [*Gaol*, p. 335, sect. 4]

Their act of sympathy only sucks them deeper into the demon
universe, for they are sympathizing with sin.

Section 5 and the rest of section 4 reveal a mind that has
been unhinged by excessive terror:

> Silently we went round and round,
> And through each hollow mind

> The Memory of dreadful things
> Rushed like a dreadful wind,
> And Horror stalked before each man,
> And Terror crept behind.
>   [*Gaol*, p. 336, sect. 4]

Wilde, his mind hollow and terror-haunted, now indulges in
a lengthy reverie in which he imagines the sin-scarred guardsman rotting in his unholy grave, his flesh and bones constantly
being eaten away. Fettered, wrapped in a sheet of flame and
eaten up by burning lime, the guardsman is not seen as
having escaped hell by dying: instead, his grave has become
his hell. Symbolically, what this means is that the fall from
grace is permanent and eternal. A sinner cannot escape hell
and be reunited with God no matter what he does. All he
can do is obtain release from consciousness by sinking into a
tomb. For three long years, we are told, no one will sow a
seed over "the unblessed spot." Throughout this section, however, there are incongruous jabs at the prison authorities, as
Reading Gaol is temporarily presented not as a symbolic but
as a literal prison.

Suddenly, Wilde recoils from his vision of horror and, yielding to the illogic of a deranged consciousness, rejects it:

> They think a murderer's heart would taint
> Each simple seed they sow.
> It is not true! God's kindly earth
> Is kindlier than men know,
> And the red rose would but blow more red,
> The white rose whiter blow.
>
> Out of his mouth a red, red rose!
> Out of his heart a white!
> For who can say by what strange way,
> Christ brings His will to light,
> Since the barren staff the pilgrim bore
> Bloomed in the great Pope's sight?
>   [*Gaol*, p. 337, sect. 4]

The assertive repetition of such key words as *kindly, white, red, blow, and rose,* plus the high incidence of alliteration and short vowels, suggests a willful refusal to face reality. These two stanzas, however, are immediately followed by two other stanzas that contradict them:

> But neither milk-white rose nor red
>   May bloom in prison air;
> The shard, the pebble, and the flint,
>   Are what they give us there:
> For flowers have been known to heal
>   A common man's despair.
>
> So never will wine-red rose or white,
>   Petal by petal, fall
> On that stretch of mud and sand that lies
>   By the hideous prison-wall,
> To tell the men who tramp the yard
>   That God's Son died for all.
>   [*Gaol,* p. 337, sect. 4]

The long syllables and negatives suggest a tired, resigned acceptance of reality. The fact that roses will never bloom over the grave clearly indicates that the guardsman is permanently damned and that God's son did not die for all. For those who have been cast out of God's universe, there is no hope of salvation, and Wilde sadly moves toward another consolation—death:

> Yet though the hideous prison-wall
>   Still hems him round and round,
> And a spirit may not walk by night
>   That is with fetters bound,
> And a spirit may but weep that lies
>   In such unholy ground,
>
> He is at peace—this wretched man—
>   At peace, or will be soon:
> There is no thing to make him mad,
>   Nor does Terror walk at noon,

> For the lampless Earth in which he lies
> Has neither Sun nor Moon.
> > [*Gaol*, p. 338, sect. 4]

The tomb is a place where peace can be found, for "the
lampless Earth" stands as a barrier between the guardsman
and the hell which is Reading Gaol, and even a spirit that
is fettered and buried in unholy ground has obtained release
from madness and terror.

The section ends with a blast of anger at the people who
hanged the guardsman—"They hanged him as a beast is
hanged"—then mellows into acceptance:

> Yet all is well; he has but passed
> To life's appointed bourne:
> > [*Gaol*, p. 339, sect. 4]

Although Wilde would like heaven to be life's appointed
bourne, he contents himself, here at any rate, with the grave.

Section 5 begins with an attack on prisons and man-made
laws, but in the fourth stanza Wilde begins to refer to prison
as hell. Then follows a long and terrifying account of the
effect of this external hell on the souls of the sinners damned
within it:

> The vilest deeds like poison weeds
> Bloom well in prison-air;
> It is only what is good in Man
> That wastes and withers there:
> Pale anguish keeps the heavy gate,
> And the Warder is Despair.
> > [*Gaol*, p. 341, sect. 5]

In this foul and dark place, the prisoners become progressively more evil until everything except "Lust, is turned to
dust."

The most terrible thing about this hell, however, is that it
destroys a person's capacity to save himself, and this by destroying his ability to feel the cleansing and purifying emotion of love:

> But though lean Hunger and green Thirst
>   Like asp with adder fight,
> We have little care of prison fare,
>   For what chills and kills outright
> Is that every stone one lifts by day
>   Becomes one's heart by night.
>   [*Gaol,* p. 342, sect. 5]

In *De Profundis,* as in the later fairy tales, the road to purity
is a "broken" heart large enough to embrace everything in
love. But where pain, terror, filth, and despair are constant
threats, one's best defense is to develop a heart of stone—to
become bitter, scornful, and unfeeling.

The ancient mariner's punishment led to his purification
and he blessed the creatures of the deep:

> A spring of love gushed from my heart,
> And I blessed them unaware:
>   [ll. 284–85]

Wilde's hell has quite the opposite effect on its inmates. In
the hell of Reading Gaol, a poisoned soul cannot purify itself: it can only become more and more foul and sin-scarred
as its ability to love is steadily eroded. And as emotions are
destroyed and the mind unhinged ("some grow mad") only the
bodily appetite of lust remains.

Wilde's vision of irrevocable damnation grows steadily
darker and more unbearable as the section continues:

> With midnight always in one's heart,
>   And twilight in one's cell,
> We turn the crank, or tear the rope,
>   Each in his separate Hell,
> And the silence is more awful far
>   Than the sound of a brazen bell.
>   [*Gaol,* p. 342, sect. 5]

In the end, Wilde reaches a point where the vision of damnation becomes unendurable and he rejects it in horror:

And thus we rust Life's iron chain
Degraded and alone:
And some men curse, and some men weep,
And some men make no moan:
But God's eternal Laws are kind
And break the heart of stone.

[*Gaol,* p. 343, sect. 5]

It is worth noting that the task of self-purification, which in
De Profundis Wilde had taken upon his own shoulders, is now
delegated to God. Whereas men actively kill the thing they
love, they seem of necessity to be passive and dependent on
God's kindness and "eternal Laws" when it comes to the task
of filling their hearts with love. The possibility of moving out
of hell, and the joy of such an occurrence, is dwelt on by
Wilde, and the section ends with him informing us that the
guardsman had purified his soul with tears of blood before he
was hanged.

The part of section 5 that speaks of purification and of
God's forgiveness, however, shows a deeply troubled mind's
recoiling from the excessive horror of the demon universe.
Throughout the poem, Wilde has stressed that God is absent
from Reading Gaol, never looking into this hell that houses
only sinners permanently cast out of His universe. Wilde presents the act of breaking the heart of stone as a passive one,
then contradicts himself by indicating that the guardsman
actively purified himself. In the first line of section 2, moreover, Wilde informs us that the guardsman stayed in Reading
Gaol for six weeks, but he now shortens the period to three.
This is possibly a mistake Wilde did not catch, but more probably the speaker's confusion about time is meant to indicate
further how deeply troubled his mind is at this stage.

That all talk of purification is an attempt to escape from a
terrible reality is proved by section 6, the last and shortest
section of the poem. In three brief stanzas, Wilde bluntly re-
affirms the idea of irrevocable damnation and undercuts the
previous section's talk of broken hearts and purified souls. The

guardsman again appears as a sinful man whose grave is a
hell, and it is reaffirmed that his fate is symbolic of the human
condition:

> In Reading Gaol by Reading town
>   There is a pit of shame,
> And in it lies a wretched man
>   Eaten by teeth of flame,
> In a burning winding-sheet he lies,
>   And his grave has got no name.
>
> And there, till Christ call forth the dead,
>   In silence let him lie:
> No need to waste the foolish tear,
>   Or heave the windy sigh:
> The man had killed the thing he loved,
>   And so he had to die.
>
> And all men kill the thing they love,
>   By all let this be heard,
> Some do it with a bitter look
>   Some with a flattering word,
> The coward does it with a kiss,
>   The brave man with a sword!
>   [*Gaol*, p. 345, sect. 6]

The guardsman in his grave is constantly being consumed
by the flames of hell. The fact that the grave has no name here
assumes symbolic proportions, for the lack of a name suggests
that it is any and every man's grave. All men kill the thing
they love, and all men, in doing so, isolate themselves in a hell
remote from God and scar their souls with sin. The phrase
"till Christ call forth the dead" is meant simply to convey re-
moteness tinged with sadness. There is no hope that a sin-
befouled soul can emerge from hell. The only possible escape
is death, and Wilde's final comment on the guardsman is a
resigned "let him lie."

The Ballad of Reading Gaol is not a perfect poem, and
Wilde was well aware of its imperfections. In October of 1897,

he wrote to Robert Ross: "With much of your criticism I agree. The poem suffers under the difficulty of a divided aim in style. Some is realistic, some is romantic: some poetry, some propaganda. I feel it keenly, but as a whole I think the production is interesting: that it is interesting from more points of view than one is artistically to be regretted" (*Letters,* p. 654). The constant swing from a realistic to a fantastic, decorative style disturbs the flow of the poem, but the more serious defect is that Wilde sometimes forgets that Reading Gaol is a symbolic hell and begins to attack prisons and human laws, seeing them as opposed to God's justice.

Thus, the poem at times becomes a propaganda leaflet in rhyme, and antiprison propaganda is quite irrelevant to the poem's main theme. Even more disturbing is that this propaganda is often confusingly mixed with dramatizations of Reading Gaol as a symbolic hell. The divided aim of *The Ballad of Reading Gaol* only confirms what *De Profundis* had already made clear—that Wilde has lost the single-minded determination necessary to produce great literature. A deeply disturbed and shattered man, he now can only write literature that reflects his chaotic state of mind and his inability to concentrate on a single theme or style.

After *The Ballad of Reading Gaol,* Oscar Wilde produced no more literature, although he did make an attempt to do so. His prison experience had shattered and destroyed him to a point where he could no longer write. Like the other decadents of the 1890s, he never managed to escape from the dark underworld he had explored and which finally claimed him. He wrote in *De Profundis:* "Many men on their release carry their prison along with them into the air, hide it as a secret disgrace in their hearts, and at length like poor poisoned things creep into some hole and die" (*Letters,* p. 470).

Wilde's letters bear ample testimony that this is precisely what happened to him. His soul, scarred with hate, bitterness, and self-pity, never managed to heal itself. Only two days before his release from prison, he wrote that he was going out "with an adder in my heart, and an asp in my tongue, and every night I sow thorns in the garden of my soul" (*Letters*, p. 554). In August, 1897, he wrote: "Nemesis has caught me in her net: to struggle is foolish" (*Letters*, p. 629). In December of the same year, he wrote: "My life cannot be patched up. There is a doom on it. Neither to myself, nor to others, am I any longer a joy" (*Letters*, p. 695). March, 1898: "My writing has gone to bits—like my character. I am simply a self-conscious nerve in pain" (*Letters*, p. 717). August, 1898: "Of course my first year in prison destroyed me body and soul. It could not have been otherwise" (*Letters*, p. 760).

After Wilde's death in November of 1900, Robert Ross wrote to Adela Schuster: "Though everyone who knew him well enough to *appreciate* his wonderful power and the sumptuous endowment of his intellect will regret his death, apart from personal affection the terrible commonplace 'it was for the best' is really true in his case" (*Letters*, p. 861).

In *The Ballad of Reading Gaol*, Wilde saw death as the only viable release from the demon universe, and it was his good fortune that death came early to him: he was only forty-six years old when he died. Much earlier, before his imprisonment, he had been in the habit of visiting Mrs. Robinson, a fashionable fortune-teller of the day, whom he used to call the Sybil of Mortimer Street. She is reported to have once said to him: "I see a very brilliant life for you up to a certain point. Then I see a wall. Beyond the wall I see nothing." [4] She was right.

In his *A Study of Oscar Wilde*, Arthur Symons wrote of Wilde that "if he might be supposed for a moment to represent anything but himself, he would be the perfect representative of all that is meant by the word 'Decadence' as used in the 'nineties' of last century and the 'noughts' of this." [5]

Wilde's emergence as a decadent is easily traceable in the development of the Sybil myth throughout his works. In "Lord Arthur Savile's Crime," Sybil is the erotic symbol of

4. Quoted in *Letters*, p. 358, n. 2.
5. Arthur Symons, *A Study of Oscar Wilde*, p. 24.

a pure state of the soul standing at the end of a long road of spiritual development, and she triumphs. In *The Picture of Dorian Gray,* on the other hand, Sybil reappears as the embodiment of a childlike purity that cannot survive the onset of maturity, and she dies. In *Salome,* Sybil is resurrected and worshiped as the terrifying pagan goddess Cybele, entirely evil and a symbol of human nature.

For the typical decadent—Dorian or Herod—the pursuit of evil beauty finally ceases to give joy and a reaction occurs. Wilde was a decadent with a deep sense of humor, and his reaction was uniquely his own. In *The Importance of Being Earnest,* he reduced the basic situations of his earlier works to the level of farce and swept them away in a loud burst of laughter. Dorian, however, had been unable to escape from the dark underworld he had explored. Alan Campbell, who had also tried to withdraw, was forced back by Dorian and brought face-to-face with a situation so terrible it finally proved unbearable. This is the typical fate of the decadent, who discovers that he has plunged too deep into the demon universe to be able to reemerge. In *De Profundis,* Wilde presents himself as trapped in a terrible underworld from which he tries to escape but fails, though he does not abandon hope of escaping at some future date.

The highly solipsistic *Ballad of Reading Gaol,* often compared to the poetry of A. E. Housman because of superficial resemblances, is really an integral part of the decadent movement, for it is a decadent's final confession that no escape from the demon universe is possible. Beardsley and the poets of the English decadence—with the exception of Symons, who reverted to Methodism after his insanity—all finally converted to Catholicism, and John Gray tried to destroy all existing copies of *Silverpoints,* his volume of decadent poetry. Wilde, however, in *The Ballad of Reading Gaol,* sees God as having permanently cast sinners out of His universe, and it is probably correct to say that, for the decadents, Christianity did not provide an escape from the demon universe but was simply an illogical temporary refuge for their deeply disturbed minds. Reluctantly, Wilde finally admitted that death affords the only release from a dark underworld grown too horrible to tolerate. If a state of mind can cause death or contribute to it, then it is perfectly true to assert that Wilde died, at least partly, because he wanted to die.

Note on References

No authoritative edition of all Wilde's writings exists. However, the many available editions are reasonably accurate, if incomplete. In my book, I have used *The Complete Works of Oscar Wilde,* edited by Robert Ross (London: Methuen, 1908). The edition is in fourteen volumes and is especially valuable because it contains a volume that brings together all Wilde's reviews and another that collects the fragments and miscellanies that Wilde produced in his lifetime. Throughout, however, I have used a very new edition of Wilde's works as a check on the 1908 Methuen edition—*The Complete Works of Oscar Wilde,* edited by J. B. Foreman (London and Glasgow: Collins, 1970). This new edition proved especially valuable in my analysis of *The Importance of Being Earnest,* for it contains the four act version of the play, which is the fullest and most complete version available.

In my analysis of *Salome,* I have used the only edition issued in English during Wilde's lifetime (London: Elkin Mathews and John Lane, and Boston: Copeland and Day, 1894). This is the only edition of the English *Salome* that can be considered authoritative.

In the case of *De Profundis,* I have used Rupert Hart-Davis's superbly edited *Letters of Oscar Wilde.* All references to Wilde's letters in the book are to Mr. Hart-Davis's collection.

Bibliography

There are several bibliographies of Oscar Wilde available. This one is simply a list of works—mainly literary—that seem to me most helpful in understanding the literature Wilde produced. The few critical and biographical works I have included are, in my opinion, the best available on Wilde.

Bentley, Eric. *The Playwright as Thinker.* New York: Reznal and Hitchcock, 1946.

Blake, William. *Complete Writings.* Edited by Geoffrey Keynes. London: Oxford University Press, 1971.

Carlyle, Thomas. *Sartor Resartus.* New York: Odyssey Press, 1937.

Charlesworth, Barbara. *Dark Passages: The Decadent Consciousness in Victorian Literature.* Madison and Milwaukee: University of Wisconsin Press, 1965.

Coleridge, Samuel Taylor. *Poetical Works.* Edited by Ernest Hartley Coleridge. London: Oxford University Press, 1969.

Dowson, Ernest. *The Poems of Ernest Dowson.* Edited by Mark Longaker. Philadelphia: University of Pennsylvania Press, 1962.

Ellmann, Richard. "Romantic Pantomime in Oscar Wilde," *Partisan Review* 30 (Fall, 1963): 342–55.

———. "Overtures to *Salome.*" In *Oscar Wilde: A Collection of Critical Essays.* Edited by Richard Ellmann. Englewood Cliffs, N.J.: Prentice-Hall, 1969.

———. "Introduction: The Artist as Critic as Wilde." In *The Artist as Critic: Critical Writings of Oscar Wilde.* Edited by Richard Ellmann. New York: Random House, 1968.

Gray, John. *Silverpoints.* London: Elkin Mathews and John Lane, 1893.

Hawthorne, Nathaniel. *The Scarlet Letter*. Philadelphia: David McKay, 1892.

Hood, Thomas. *Poetical Works*. London: Oxford Edition, 1906.

Hough, Graham. *The Last Romantics*. London: Gerald Duckworth, 1949.

Huysmans, J.-K. *À Rebours*. Paris: Fasquelle Éditeurs, 1934.

Jackson, Holbrook. *The Eighteen Nineties*. New York: Alfred A. Knopf, 1922.

Johnson, Lionel. *Poetical Works of Lionel Johnson*. London: Elkin Mathews, and New York: Macmillan, 1915.

Keats, John. *Poetical Works*. Edited by H. W. Garrod. London: Oxford University Press, 1970.

Pater, Walter. Standard Edition. *The Renaissance: Studies in Art and Poetry*. London: Macmillan, 1907.

Pearson, Hesketh. *The Life of Oscar Wilde*. London: Methuen, 1954.

Rossetti, Dante Gabriel. *The Collected Works*. Edited by William M. Rossetti. London: Ellis, 1911.

San Juan, Jr., Epifanio. *The Art of Oscar Wilde*. Princeton, N.J.: Princeton University Press, 1967.

Shelley, Percy Bysshe. *Poetical Works*. Edited by Thomas Hutchinson. London: Oxford University Press, 1970.

Symons, Arthur. *Silhouettes*. London: Elkin Mathews and John Lane, 1892.

———. *London Nights*. London: Leonard C. Smithers, 1895.

———. *Poems*. 2 vols. London: William Heinemann, 1924.

———. *A Study of Oscar Wilde*. London: Charles J. Sawyer, 1930.

Tennyson, Alfred. *Poetical Works*. Edited by Geoffrey Cumberlege. London: Oxford University Press, 1953.

Wilde, Oscar. *Complete Works*. 14 vols. Edited by Robert Ross. London: Methuen, 1908.

———. *Complete Works*. Edited by J. B. Foreman. London and Glasgow: Collins, 1970.

———. *Salome*. London: Elkin Mathews and John Lane, and Boston: Copeland and Day, 1894.

————. *The Letters of Oscar Wilde.* Edited by Rupert Hart-Davis. New York: Harcourt, Brace and World, 1962.

Wordsworth, William. *Poetical Works.* Edited by Thomas Hutchinson. London: Oxford University Press, 1969.

Index

(Excludes introduction, footnotes, and bibliography)